Nick Vandome

Mac OS X
Lion

in easy steps

In easy steps is an imprint of In Easy Steps Limited
4 Chapel Court · 42 Holly Walk · Leamington Spa
Warwickshire · United Kingdom · CV32 4YS
www.ineasysteps.com

Notice of Liability

Every effort has been made to ensure that this book contains accurate
and current information. However, In Easy Steps Limited and the
author shall not be liable for any loss or damage suffered by readers
as a result of any information contained herein.

Trademarks

Mac OS X® is a registered trademark of Apple Computer, Inc. All
other trademarks are acknowledged as belonging to their respective
companies.

In Easy Steps Limited supports The Forest Stewardship Council (FSC),
the leading international forest certification organisation. All our titles
that are printed on Greenpeace approved FSC certified paper carry the
FSC logo.

Mixed Sources
Product group from well-managed
forests and other controlled sources
www.fsc.org   Cert no. SGS-COC-005998
© 1996 Forest Stewardship Council

Printed and bound in the United Kingdom

ISBN 978-1-84078-439-8

Contents

1 Introducing Lion

Lion is the latest operating system from Apple Computers. It is not only enjoyable and secure to use, it also has a raft of innovative features that transform a number of traditional ways for using computers. This chapter introduces the OS X interface and shows how to get started with it.

About OS X Lion

OS X Lion is the seventh version (10.7) of the operating system for Apple computers; the iMac, MacBook, Mac Mini and Mac Pro. When OS X (pronounced 'ten') was first introduced it was a major breakthrough in terms of ease of use and stability. It is based on the UNIX programming language, that is a very stable and secure operating environment and ensures that OS X is one of the most stable consumer operating systems that has ever been designed. More importantly for the user, it is also one of the most stylish and user-friendly operating systems available.

Through the previous six versions of OS X it has been refined and improved in terms of both performance and functionality. This process continues with OS X Lion, but there are also a number of revolutionary features that are unique to any operating system.

Some of the new features in OS X Lion are innovative in that they have been inspired by the functionality of Apple's mobile devices: iPhone, iPod touch and iPad, rather than vice versa. The two main areas where the functionality of the mobile devices has been transferred to the desktop and laptop operating system are:

- The way programs can be downloaded and installed. Instead of using a disc, OS X Lion utilizes the Mac App Store to provide programs, which can be installed in a couple of simple steps

- Options for navigating around pages and applications on a trackpad or a Magic Mouse. Instead of having to use a mouse or a traditional laptop trackpad, OS X Lion allows new Multi-Touch Gestures that provide a range of ways for accessing programs, apps and web pages and navigating around them

OS X Lion also addresses another area that has been a constant annoyance for computer users: the loss of work or information if your computer crashes while you are working on a document. OS X Lion solves this problem with a new function that will automatically save your work in the background, without you having to worry about it.

In many ways OS X Lion is a genuinely revolutionary operating system and, with its range of functions and innovations, it can justifiably claim to be in a position to radically change the way in which people work and interact with their Macs.

Don't forget

UNIX is an operating system that has traditionally been used for large commercial mainframe computers. It is renowned for its stability and ability to be used within different computing environments.

Installing OS X Lion

One of the many new innovations in OS X Lion is the way that programs can be downloaded and installed. Traditionally, this has been done with an installation CD or DVD, but OS X Lion changes this by providing programs for downloading directly from the online Mac App Store. This also includes obtaining OS X Lion itself. New Macs will have Lion installed but if you want to install it on an existing Mac you will need to have a minimum requirement of:

- OS X Snow Leopard (version 10.6.8)

- Intel Core 2 Duo, Core i3, Core i5, Core i7, or Xeon processor

- 2Gb of memory

If your Mac meets these requirements, you can download and install OS X Lion as follows:

1. Click on this icon on the Dock to access the App Store

2. Locate the Lion icon and click on the Install button to begin the installation process

Don't forget

The installation of OS X Lion usually takes a minimum of 30 minutes, depending on the power and speed of your Mac.

3. Follow the installation screens including one for where OS X Lion is installed (this is usually the Mac Hard Disk)

Mac OS X Lion

Mac OS X will be installed on the disk "Macintosh HD".

Macintosh HD

← →
Back Install

The OS X Environment

The first most noticeable element about OS X is its elegant user interface. This has been designed to create a user friendly graphic overlay to the UNIX operating system at the heart of OS X and it is a combination of rich colors and sharp, original graphics. The main elements that make up the initial OS X environment are:

Apple menu   Menu bar   Windows

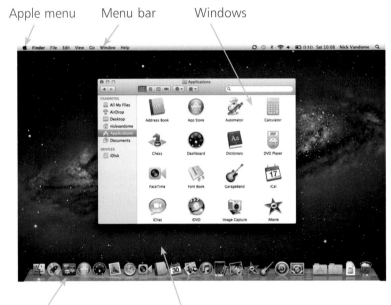

The Dock   Desktop

The Apple menu is standardized throughout OS X, regardless of the program in use

Hot tip

The Dock is designed to help make organizing and opening items as quick and easy as possible. For a detailed look at the Dock, see Chapter Two.

Aqua Interface

The name given by Apple to its OS X interface is Aqua. This describes the graphical appearance of the operating system. Essentially, it is just the cosmetic appearance of the elements within the operating system, but they combine to give OS X a rich visual look and feel. Some of the main elements of the Aqua interface are:

Menus

Menus in OS X contain commands for the operating system and any relevant programs. If there is an arrow next to a command it means there are subsequent options for the item:

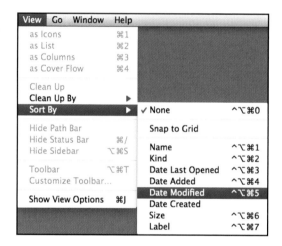

Don't forget

The graphics used in OS X are designed in a style known as Quartz. The design of this means that some elements, such as menus, allow the background behind them to show through.

Window buttons

These appear in any open OS X window and can be used to manipulate the window.

Option buttons

Whenever a dialog box with separate options is accessed, OS X highlights the suggested option with a pulsing blue button. This can be accepted by clicking on it or by pressing Enter. If you do not want to accept this option, click on another button in the dialog box.

Don't forget

The red window button is used to close a window. However, this does not quit the program. The amber button is used to minimize a window and the green one is used to expand a window.

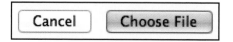

About Your Mac

When you buy a new Mac you will almost certainly check the technical specifications before you make a purchase. Once you have your Mac, there will be times when you will want to view these specifications again, such as the version of OS X in use, the amount of memory and the amount of storage. This can be done through the About This Mac option that can be accessed from the Apple Menu. To do this:

1 Click on the Apple Menu and click on the About This Mac link

2 The About This Mac window has information about the version of OS X, the processor, the memory and the Startup Disk being used

Don't forget

For more information about Software Updates, see Chapter Eleven.

3 Click on Software Update... button to see available software updates for your Mac

4 Click on the More Info... button to view more About This Mac options

Overview

This gives additional general information about your Mac:

① Click on the Overview button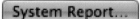

② This window contains additional information such as the type of graphics card and the Serial Number

③ Click on the System Report... button to view full details about the hardware and software on your Mac

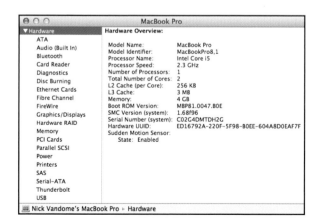

④ Click on the Check for Updates... button to view available software updates for your Mac

...cont'd

Display information

This gives information about your Mac's display:

 Click on the Displays button   **Displays**

 This window contains information about your display including the type, size, resolution and graphics card

Built-in Color LCD Display

13-inch (1280 x 800)

Intel HD Graphics 3000 384 MB graphics

Displays Preferences...

 Click on the Displays Preferences…   **Displays Preferences...**

button to view options for changing the display's resolution, brightness and color

 Don't forget

For more information about changing the resolution, see page 20.

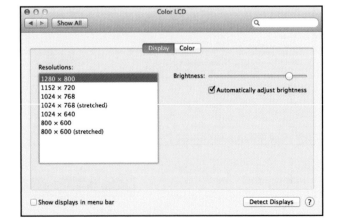

14

Storage information

This contains information about your Mac's physical and removable storage:

1 Click on the Storage button

2 This window contains information about the used and available storage on your hard disk and also options for writing various types of CDs and DVDs

The disk usage is shown for different content types on your Mac e.g. videos, music, photos and applications.

3 Click on the Disk Utility... button to view options for repairing problems on your Mac

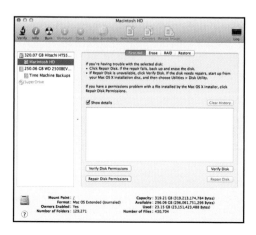

15

Memory information

This contains information about your Mac's memory, that is used to run OS X and also the applications on your computer:

1 Click on the Memory button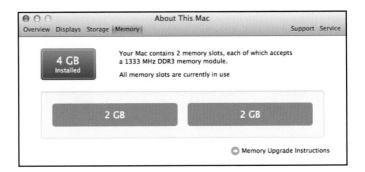

2 This window contains information about the memory chips that are in your Mac

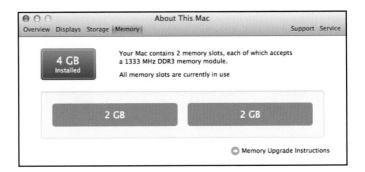

3 Click on the Memory Upgrade Instructions if you want to upgrade your memory chips

4 A page on the Apple website gives instructions for upgrading memory chips for different makes and models of Macs

Beware

Always wear an anti-static wristband if you are opening your Mac to insert new memory chips, or any other time when you are working on the components of your Mac.

About System Preferences

OS X Lion has a wide range of options for customizing and configuring the way that your Mac operates. These are located within the Systems Preferences section. To access this:

1 Click on this button on the Dock (the bar of icons that appears along the bottom of the screen), or from the Applications folder

Don't forget

For more detailed information about the Dock, see Chapter Two.

2 All of the options are shown in the System Preferences window

Don't forget

For a detailed look at the System Preferences, see Chapter Two.

3 Click once on an item to open it in the main System Preferences window. Each item will have a number of options for customizing it

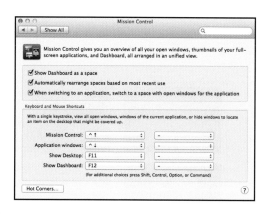

4 Click on the Show All button to return to the main System Preferences window

Changing the Background

Background imagery is an important way to add your own personal touch to your Mac. (This is the graphical element upon which all other items on your computer sit.) There are a range of background options that can be used. To select your own background:

You can select your own photographs as your desktop background, once you have loaded them onto your Mac. To do this, select the iPhoto folder and browse to the photograph you want.

1 Click on this button in the System Preferences folder

Desktop & Screen Saver

2 Click on the Desktop tab

Desktop

3 Select a location from where you want to select a background

▼ Apple
　📁 Desktop Pictures
　📁 Nature
　📁 Plants
　📁 Art
　📁 Black & White
　📁 Abstract
　📁 Patterns
　⚫ Solid Colors

4 Click on one of the available backgrounds

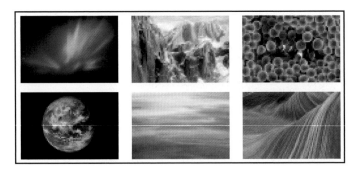

5 The background is applied as the desktop background imagery

Changing the Screen Saver

A screen saver is the element that appears when the Mac has not been used for a specified period of time. Originally this was designed to avoid screen burn (caused by items being at the same position on the screen for an extended period of time) but now they largely consist of a graphical element. To select your own screen saver:

1 Click on this button in the System Preferences folder

Desktop & Screen Saver

2 Click on the Screen Saver tab

Screen Saver

Don't forget

Screen savers were originally designed to prevent screen burn (areas of the screen becoming marked as a result of elements remaining static for a prolonged period of time), but now they are more for cosmetic graphical purposes.

3 Select a location from where you want to select a screen saver

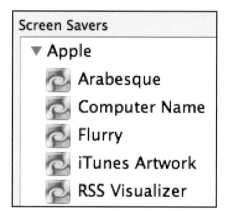

Screen Savers

▼ Apple
- Arabesque
- Computer Name
- Flurry
- iTunes Artwork
- RSS Visualizer

4 Click the Test button to preview the selected screen saver

Test

5 Drag this slider to specify the amount of time the Mac is inactive before the screen saver is activated

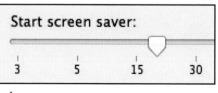

Start screen saver:

3   5   15   30

Changing the Resolution

For most computer users the size at which items are displayed on the screen is a crucial issue: if items are too small this can make them hard to read and lead to eye strain; too large and you have to spend a lot of time scrolling around to see everything.

The size of items on the screen is controlled by the screen's resolution, i.e. the number of colored dots displayed in an area of the screen. The higher the resolution the smaller the items on the screen, the lower the resolution the larger the items. To change the screen resolution:

Don't forget

A higher resolution makes items appear sharper on the screen, even though they appear physically smaller.

20

1 Click on this button in the System Preferences folder

Displays

2 Click on the Display tab

Display

3 Select a resolution setting to change the overall screen resolution

Resolutions:

1280 × 800
1152 × 720
1024 × 768
1024 × 768 (stretched)
1024 × 640

4 Drag this slider to change the screen brightness. Check on the box to have this done automatically for the current lighting conditions, via an ambient light sensor (if fitted)

Brightness: ⎯⎯⎯⎯⎯⎯⎯⎯⎯⎯◯⎯⎯

☑ **Automatically adjust brightness**

5 Click on the Color tab to select options for using different color profiles and also calibrating your monitor

Color

Universal Access

In all areas of computing it is important to give as many people access to the system as possible. This includes users with visual impairments and also people who have problems using the mouse and keyboard. In OS X this is achieved through the functions of the Universal Access System Preferences. To use these:

1 Click on the this button in the System Preferences folder

2 Click on the Seeing tab for help with issues connected with visual impairment

3 Check on the Zoom On button to enable zooming in on specific areas of the screen

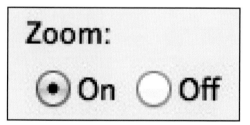

4 Check on the White on Black display button to invert the default settings for your system display

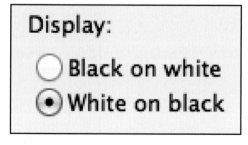

Don't forget

Experiment with the VoiceOver function (in the Seeing window) if only to see how it operates. This will give you a better idea of how visually impaired users access information on a computer.

...cont'd

5 Click on the Hearing tab to adjust settings for audio problem

Hearing

6 Click on this button to adjust the system volume

Adjust Volume...

7 Check on this box to make the screen flash whenever there is a sound alert on your Mac

☑ **Flash the screen when an alert sound occurs**
Test the screen flash: **Flash Screen**

Don't forget

Under the Keyboard tab there are options for the time it takes for a keystroke to appear on the screen and how long before a keystroke is repeated if a key is held down for a few seconds.

8 Click on the Keyboard tab to access options for customizing your keyboard

Keyboard

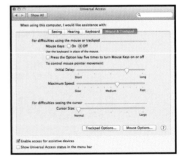

9 Click on the Mouse & Trackpad tab to access options for customizing these devices

Mouse & Trackpad

Background on UNIX

UNIX is the powerful and robust operating system that is the foundation on which OS X runs. In fact, OS X is essentially a very impressive graphical interface placed on top of a version of UNIX known as Darwin.

UNIX was developed in the early 1970s by programmers who wanted to design an operating system that could run on any platform, i.e. different types of computers. Up until then, each operating system had generally been designed for a specific type of computer. Another benefit of UNIX was that it was designed to be available to the whole development community. The program that was used to create UNIX is the now widely used C language.

UNIX first gained popularity in academic institutions and it was then taken on by government organizations. Its adoption by Apple as the foundation for OS X has seen UNIX move into the mainstream of consumer computing. UNIX's greatest strength is its stability, while its greatest weakness is perhaps its non-user-friendliness. Apple have made the most of the former and overcome the latter with its Aqua interface and Quartz graphics.

For people with experience of UNIX, programming can be performed within OS X in the Terminal window. This is the gateway into the UNIX environment and it can be located in the Applications>Utilities folder.

Don't forget

In addition to OS X on consumer computers Apple have also released a server that runs on UNIX. This is called Lion Server and it is used to run and manage computer networks.

Terminal

If you are not familiar with UNIX, you need never worry about it or the Terminal again.

Shutting Down

The Apple menu (which can be accessed by clicking on the Apple icon at the top left corner of the desktop or any subsequent OS X window) has been standardized in OS X. This means that it has the same options regardless of the program in which you are working. This has a number of advantages, not least is the fact that it makes it easier to shut down your Mac. When shutting down, there are three options that can be selected:

- Sleep. This puts the Mac into hibernation mode, i.e. the screen goes blank and the hard drive becomes inactive. This state is maintained until the mouse is moved or a key is pressed on the keyboard. This then wakes up the Mac and it is ready to continue work

- Restart. This closes down the Mac and then restarts it again. This can be useful if you have added new software and your computer requires a restart to make it active

- Shut Down. This closes down the Mac completely once you have finished working

Click here to access the Apple menu

Click here to access one of the shut down options

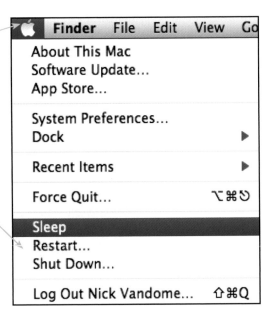

2 Getting Up and Running

This chapter looks at some of the essential features of OS X. These include the Dock for organizing and accessing all of the elements of the computer, the system preferences for the way the computer looks and operates and items for arranging folders and files.

Introducing the Dock

The Dock is one of the main organizational elements of OS X. Its main function is to help organize and access programs, folders and files. In addition, with its rich translucent colors and elegant graphical icons, it also makes an aesthetically pleasing addition to the desktop. The main things to remember about the Dock are:

- It is divided into two: programs go on the left of the dividing line; all other items go on the right

- It can be edited in just about any way you choose

By default the Dock appears at the bottom of the screen

Programs go here   Dividing line   Open items

If a progam window is closed, the program remains open and the window is placed within the progam icon on the Dock. If an item is minimized it goes on the right of the Dock dividing line.

Don't forget

The Dock is always displayed as a line of icons, but this can be orientated either vertically or horizontally.

Hot tip

Items on the Dock can be opened by clicking on them once, rather than having to double-click on them. Once they have been accessed the icon bobs up and down until the item is available.

Setting Dock Preferences

As with most elements of OS X, the Dock can be modified in numerous ways. This can affect both the appearance of the Dock and the way it operates. To set Dock preferences:

1 Select Apple Menu>Dock from the Menu bar

> Turn Hiding On   ⌥⌘D
> Turn Magnification On
>
> Position on Left
> ✓ Position on Bottom
> Position on Right
>
> Dock Preferences...

2 Select the general preferences here

Dock Preferences...

3 Click here to access more Dock preferences (below)

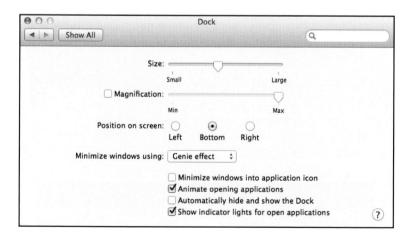

Hot tip

The Apple Menu is constantly available in OS X, regardless of the program in which you are working. The menu options are also constant in all applications.

Beware

You will not be able to make the Dock size too large so that some of the icons would not be visible on the desktop. By default, the Dock is resized so that everything is always visible.

...cont'd

The Dock Preferences allow you to change its size, orientation, the way icons appear and effects for when items are minimized:

The "Position on screen" options enable you to place the Dock on the left, right or bottom of the screen

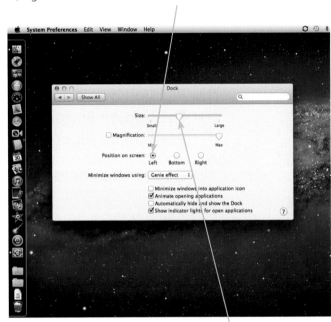

Drag the Dock Size slider to increase or decrease the size of the Dock

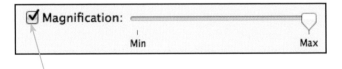

Check on the Magnification box and drag the slider to determine the size to which icons are enlarged when the cursor is moved over them

The effects that are applied to items when they are minimized is one of the features of OS X (it is not absolutely necessary but it sums up the Apple ethos of trying to enhance the user experience as much as possible).

The Genie effect shrinks the item to be minimized like a genie going back into its lamp

Hot tip

Open windows can also be minimized by double-clicking on their title bar (the thinly lined bar at the top of the window, next to the three window buttons.)

Manual resizing

In addition to changing the size of the Dock by using the Dock Preference dialog box, it can also be resized manually:

Drag vertically on the Dock dividing line to increase or decrease its size

Stacks on the Dock

Stacking items

To save space on the Dock it is possible to add folders to the Dock, from where their contents can be accessed. This is known as Stacks. By default, Stacks for documents and downloaded files are created on the Dock. To use Stacks:

1 Stacked items are placed on the right of the Dock dividing line

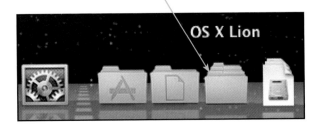

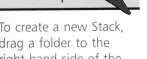

Hot tip

To create a new Stack, drag a folder to the right-hand side of the Dock, i.e. to the right of the dividing line.

2 Click on a Stack to view its contents

3 Stacks can be viewed as a grid, or

4 As a fan, depending on the number of items it contains

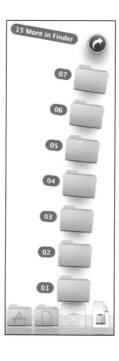

Hot tip

Move the cursor over a stack and press Ctrl+click to access options for how that stack is displayed.

5 Click on a folder to view its contents within a Stack. Click on files to open them in their relevant program

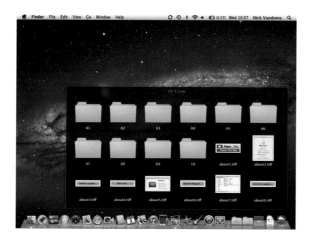

6 To create a new Stack, drag a folder onto the Dock. Any new items that are added to the folder will also be visible through the Stack

Dock Menus

One of the features of the Dock is that it can display contextual menus for selected items. This means that it shows menus with options that are applicable to the item that is being accessed. This can only be done when an item has been opened.

1 Click and hold here to display an item's individual menu

Hot tip

Click on Quit on the Dock's contextual menu to close an open program or file, depending on which side of the dividing bar the item is located.

2 Click on Show in Finder to see where the item is located on your computer

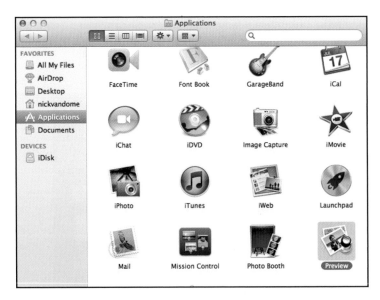

Working with Dock Items

Adding items

As many items as you like can be added to the Dock; the only restriction is the size of monitor in which to display all of the Dock items (the size of the Dock can be reduced to accommodate more icons but you have to be careful that all of the icons are still legible). To add items to the Dock:

Locate the required item and drag it onto the Dock. All of the other icons move along to make space for the new one

Don't forget

Icons on the Dock are shortcuts to the related item, rather than the item itself, which remains in its original location.

Keep in Dock

Every time you open a new program, its icon will appear in the Dock for the duration that the program is open, even if it has not previously been put in the Dock. If you then decide that you would like to keep it in the Dock, you can do so as follows:

Beware

You can add as many items as you like to the Dock, but it will automatically shrink to display all of its items if it becomes too big for the available space.

1 Click and hold on the icon underneath an open program

2 Click on Keep In Dock to ensure the program remains in the Dock when it is closed

...cont'd

Removing items

Any item, except the Finder, can be removed from the Dock. However, this does not remove it from our computer, it just removes the shortcut for accessing it. You will still be able to locate it in its folder on your hard drive and, if required, drag it back onto the Dock. To remove items from the Dock:

Drag it away from the Dock and release. The item disappears in a satisfying puff of smoke to indicate that it has been removed. All of the other icons then move up to fill in the space

Removing open programs

You can remove a program from the Dock, even if it is open and running. To do this:

1. Drag a program off the Dock while it is running. Initially the icon will remain on the Dock because the program is still open

2. When the program is closed its icon will be removed from the Dock (unless Keep in Dock has been selected from the item's Dock menu)

Trash

The Trash folder is a location for placing items that you do not want to use anymore. However, when items are placed in the Trash, they are not removed from your computer. This requires another command, as the Trash is really a holding area before you decide you want to remove items permanently. The Trash can also be used for ejecting removable disks attached to your Mac.

Sending items to the Trash

Items can be sent to the Trash by dragging them from the location in which they are stored:

1 Drag an item over the Trash icon to place it in the Trash folder

2 Click once on the Trash icon on the Dock to view its contents

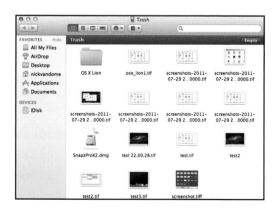

Don't forget

Items can also be sent to the Trash by selecting them and then selecting File>Move to Trash from the Menu bar.

Don't forget

All of the items within the Trash can be removed in a single command: Select Finder>Empty Trash from the Menu bar to remove all of the items in the Trash folder.

System Preferences

In OS X there are preferences that can be set for just about every aspect of the program. This gives you great control over how the interface looks and how the operating system functions. To access System Preferences:

Click on this icon on the Dock or from the Applications folder in the Finder

Personal preferences

General. Options for the overall look of buttons, menus, windows and scroll bars.

Desktop & Screen Saver. This can be used to change the desktop background and the screen saver.

Dock. Options for the way the Dock looks and functions.

Mission Control This gives you variety of options for managing all of your open windows and programs.

Language & Text. Options for the language used on the computer.

Security &Privacy. This enables you to secure your Home folder with a master password, for added security.

Spotlight. This can be used to specify settings for the OS X search facility, Spotlight

Universal Access. This can be used to set options for users who have difficulty with viewing text on screen, hearing commands, using the keyboard or using the mouse.

Hardware preferences

CDs & DVDs. Options for what action is taken when you insert CDs and DVDs.

Displays. Options for the screen display, such as resolution.

Energy Saver. Options for when the computer is inactive.

Keyboard. Options for how the keyboard functions and also keyboard shortcuts.

Mouse. Options for how the mouse functions.

Trackpad. Options for if you are using a trackpad

Print & Scan. Options for selecting printers and scanners.

Sound. Options for adding sound effects and playing and recording sound.

Internet & Wireless preferences

Mail, Contacts & Calendars. This can be used to set up contacts on your Mac, using a variety of online services.

MobileMe. Options for the online MobileMe service. However, this is being replaced by iCloud in fall/autumn 2011

Network. This can be used to specify network settings for linking two or more computers together. This is covered in more detail in Chapter Nine.

Bluetooth. Options for attaching Bluetooth wireless devices

Sharing. This can be used to specify how files are shared over a network. This is also covered in Chapter Nine.

System preferences

Users & Groups. This can be used to allow different users to create their own accounts for use on the same computer.

Date & Time. Options for changing the computer's date and time to time zones around the world.

Parental Controls. This can be used to limit access to the computer and various online functions.

Software Update. This can be used to specify how software updates are handled. It can be set so that updates are automatically downloaded when the computer is connected to the Internet, or they can be done manually.

Speech. Options for using speakable commands to control the computer.

Startup Disk. This can be used to specify the disk from which your computer starts up. This is usually the OS X volume.

Time Machine. This can be used to configure and set up the OS X backup facility.

Desktop Items

If required, the Desktop can be used to store programs and files. However, the Finder (see Chapter Three) does such a good job of organizing all of the elements within your computer that the Desktop is rendered largely redundant, unless you feel happier storing items here. The Desktop also displays any removable disks that are connected to your computer:

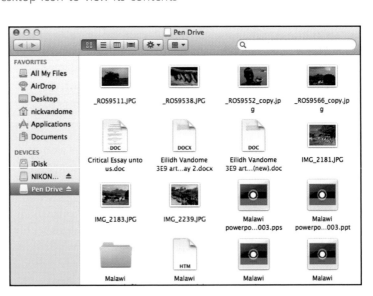

NIKON D200

Pen Drive

Hot tip

Icons for removable disks, i.e. pen drives, CDs or DVDs, will only become visible on the Desktop once a disk has been inserted into the appropriate drive.

If a removable disk is connected to your computer, double-click the Desktop icon to view its contents

Don't forget

Any removable disks that are connected to your computer can also be viewed by clicking on them in the Sidebar in the Finder.

Ejecting Items

If you have removable disks attached to your Mac it is essential
to be able to eject them quickly and easily. In OS X there are two
ways in which this can be done:

1 In the Finder, click on the icon
to the right of the name of the
removable disk

2 On the Desktop, drag the disk icon
over the Trash. This turns the Trash
icon into the Eject icon and the disk
will be ejected

3 Some disks, such as CDs and DVDs are physically ejected
when either of these two action are performed. Other
disks, such as pen drives, have to be removed manually
once they have been ejected by OS X. If the disk is not
ejected first the following warning message will appear:

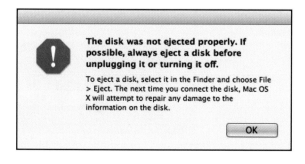

Auto Save and Versions

One of the biggest causes of frustration when working with computers is if they crash and all of your unsaved work is lost. Luckily, with OS X Lion, losing unsaved material is now a thing of the past as it includes an Auto Save function that saves work in the background as you go along. This means that you do not have to worry about having unsaved documents.

Another function within Auto Save is Versions, which enables you to revert back to previous versions of a document. To do this:

Don't forget

The Save a Version option is used instead of the standard Save function. Each time it is used it saves a new version of the current document or file.

1 Create a document with content

2 Select File>Save a Version from the Menu bar

3 Edit the file

4 Click on the
file name and
select Browse All
Versions...

5 The current version is shown on the left-hand side and
the previous versions on the right

Hot tip

To prevent any more
changes being made to
a document, click on the
file name and click on
Lock. To keep the current
version and use another
for editing, click on the
Duplicate link.

6 Click on a
previous version

7 Click on the Restore button

8 The
previous
version is
restored as
the current
document

41

Resuming

One of the chores about computing is that when you close down your computer you have to first close down all of your open documents and programs and then open them all again when you turn your machine back on again. However, OS X Lion has an innovative feature that allows you to continue working exactly where you left off, even if you turn off your computer. To do this:

1 Before you close down all of your open documents and programs will be available

2 Select the Shut Down or Restart option from the Apple menu

3 Make sure this box is checked on (this will ensure that all of you items will appear as before once the Mac is closed down and then opened again)

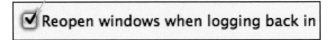

4 Confirm the Shut Down or Restart command

3 Finder

The principal program for moving around OS X is the Finder. This enables you to access items and organize your programs, folders and files. This chapter looks at how to use the Finder and how to get the most out of this powerful tool that is at the heart of navigating around OS X. It covers accessing items through the Finder, how to customize the interface and numerous options for working with folders in OS X.

Working with the Finder

If you were only able to use one item on the Dock it would be the Finder. This is the gateway to all of the elements of your computer. It is possible to get to selected items through other routes, but the Finder is the only location where you can gain access to everything on your system. If you ever feel that you are getting lost within OS X, click on the Finder and then you should begin to feel more at home. To access the Finder:

Click once on this icon on the Dock

Overview

The Finder has its own toolbar, a Sidebar from which items can be accessed and a main window where the contents of selected items can be viewed:

Forward and back   View options   Actions button   Search

View all files

Folders are displayed here

Sidebar

Main windows

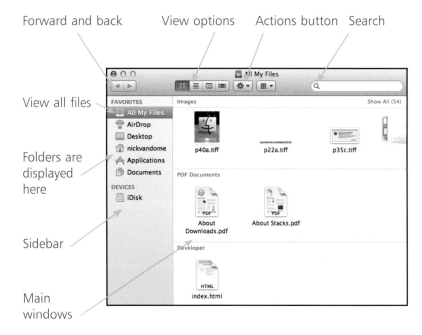

Finder Folders

All My Files

This contains all of the latest files on which you have been working. They are sorted into categories according to file type so that you can search through them quickly. This is an excellent way to locate items without having to look through a lot of folders. To access this:

1 Click on this link in the Finder Sidebar to access the contents of your All My Files folder

2 All of your files are displayed in individual categories. Click on the headings at the top of each category to sort items by that criteria

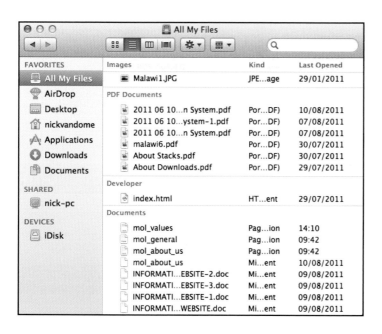

Don't forget

Under Devices in the Finder Sidebar is the iDisk. This is an online facility for storing and backing up your files. At present it is used with the MobileMe service but, from fall/autumn 2011, this will be replaced by the iCloud service and iDisk will only be available until June 30 2012. To use iDisk you simply drag and drop files onto it in the Finder Sidebar and then they are uploaded to the online iDisk.

...cont'd

Home folder

This contains the contents of your own home directory, containing your personal folders and files. OS X inserts some pre-named folders which it thinks will be useful, but it is possible to rename, rearrange or delete these as you please. It is also possible to add as many more folders as you want.

1   Click on this link to access the contents of your Home folder

2   The Home folder contains the Public folder that can be used to share files with other users if the computer is part of a network

Hot tip

When you are creating documents OS X, by default, recognizes their type and then, when you save them, suggests the most applicable folder in your Home directory in which to save them. So, if you have created a word processed document, OS X will suggest you save it in Documents, if it is a photograph it will suggest Pictures, if it is a video it will suggest Movies, and so on.

Applications

This folder contains all of the applications on your Mac. They can also be accessed from the Launchpad as shown in Chapter Five.

Downloads

This is the default folder for any files or programs that you download (other than those from the Apple App Store).

Documents

This is part of your home folder but is put on the Finder Sidebar for ease of access. New folders can be created for different types of documents.

Finder Views

The way in which items are displayed within the Finder can be amended in a variety of ways, depending on how you want to view the contents of a folder. Different folders can have their own viewing options applied to them and these will stay in place until a new option is specified.

Back button

When working within the Finder each new window replaces the previous one, unless you open a new program. This prevents the screen becoming cluttered with dozens of open windows, as you look through various Finder windows for a particular item. To ensure that you never feel lost within the Finder structure, there is a Back button on the Finder toolbar that enables you to retrace the steps that you have taken.

Beware

If you have not opened any Finder windows, the Back button will not operate at all.

1   Navigate to a folder within the Finder (in this case the "For printing" folder contained within Pictures)

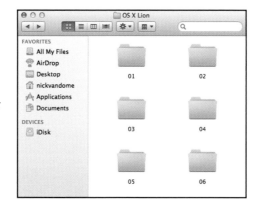

Hot tip

Select an item within the Finder window and click on the space bar to view its details.

2   Click on the Back button to move back to the previously visited window (in this case, the main Pictures window)

Icon view

One of the viewing options for displaying items within the Finder is as icons. This provides a graphical representation of the items in the Finder. It is possible to customize the way that Icon view looks and functions:

Hot tip

The Arrange By options can be used to arrange icons into specific groups, e.g. by name or type, or to snap them to an invisible grid so that they have an ordered appearance.

1 Click here on the Finder toolbar to access Icon view

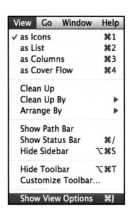

2 Select View from the Menu bar, check on "as Icons" and select "Show View Options" to access the options for customizing Icon view

Hot tip

A very large icon size can be useful for people with poor eyesight, but it does take up a lot more space in a window.

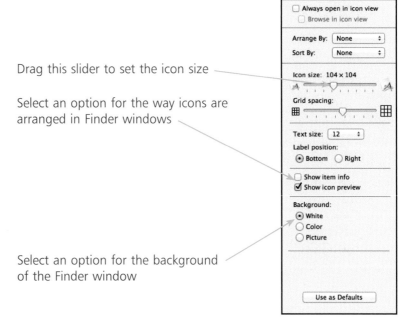

Drag this slider to set the icon size

Select an option for the way icons are arranged in Finder windows

Select an option for the background of the Finder window

List view

List view can be used to show the items within a Finder window as a list, with additional information shown next to them. This can be a more efficient method than icon view if there are a lot of items within a folder; List view enables you to see more items at one time and also view the additional information.

1. Click here on the Finder toolbar to access List view

2. The name of each folder or file is displayed here. If any item has additional elements within it, this is represented by a small triangle next to them. Additional information in List view, such as file size and last modified date, is included in columns to the right

Column view

Column view is a useful option if you want to trace the location of a particular item, i.e. see the full path of its location, starting from the hard drive.

1. Click here on the Finder toolbar to access Column view

2. Click on an item to see everything within that folder. If an arrow follows an item it means that there are further items to view

49

Covers

Covers is another innovative feature on the Mac, that enables you to view items as large icons. This is particularly useful for image files as it enables you to quickly see the details of the image to see if it is the one you want. To use Covers:

1 Select a folder and at the top of the Finder window click on this button

2 The items within the folder are displayed in their cover state

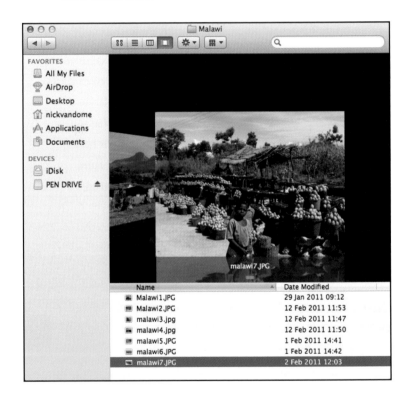

3 Drag with the mouse on each item to view the next one, or click on the slider at the bottom of the window. You can also move between items by swiping left or right on a trackpad or Magic Mouse

Quick Look

Through a Finder option called Quick Look, it is possible to view the content of a file without having to first open it. To do this:

1   Select a file within the Finder

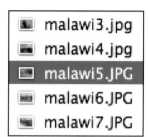

Hot tip

In Quick Look it is even possible to preview videos or presentations without having to first open them in their default program.

2   Press the space bar

3   The contents of the file are displayed without it opening in its default program

4   Click on the cross to close Quick Look

Finder Toolbar

Customizing the toolbar

As with most elements of OS X, it is possible to customize the Finder toolbar:

1 Select View>Customize Toolbar from the Menu bar

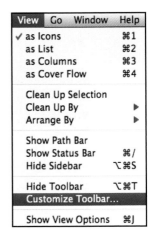

2 Drag items from the window into the toolbar, or:

3 Drag the default set of icons into the toolbar

4 Click Done at the bottom of the window

Finder Sidebar

Using the Sidebar

The Sidebar is the left-hand panel of the Finder which can be used to access items on your Mac:

1 Click on a button on the Sidebar

2 Its contents are displayed in the main Finder window

Don't forget

When you click on an item in the Sidebar, its contents are shown in the main Finder window to its right.

Adding to the Sidebar

Items that you access most frequently can be added to the Sidebar. To do this:

Don't forget

When items are added to the Finder Sidebar a shortcut, or alias, is inserted into the Sidebar, not the actual item.

1 Drag an item from the main Finder window onto the Sidebar

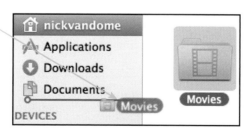

Don't forget

Items can be removed from the Sidebar by Ctrl+clicking on them and selecting Remove from Sidebar from the contextual menu.

2 The item is added to the Sidebar. You can do this with programs, folders and files

Finder Search

Searching electronic data is now a massive industry, with companies such as Google leading the way with online searching. On Macs it is also possible to search your folders and files, using the built-in search facilities. This can be done either through the Finder or with the Spotlight program (see Chapter Six).

Using Finder

To search for items within the Finder:

Don't forget

Try and make your search keywords and phrases as accurate as possible. This will create a better list of search results.

1 In the Finder window, enter the search keyword(s) in this box. Search options are listed below the keyword

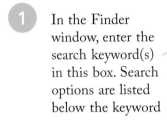

2 Select an option for what you search over

3 In the Search box click on the token next to the keyword. This gives you additional options for what to search over

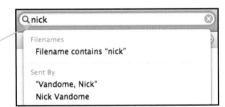

4 The search results are shown in the Finder window

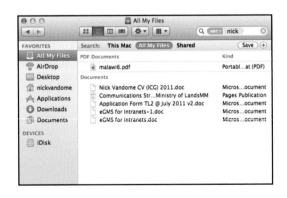

Don't forget

Both folders and files will be displayed in the Finder as part of the search results.

5 Double-click on a file to open it

Creating Aliases

Aliases are shortcuts to the actual version of items. This can include programs, folders and files. Aliases take up virtually no disk space and numerous aliases can be created for a single item and then placed in various locations for ease of access. To create an alias:

1 Select an item in any open window, by clicking on it once

2 Select File>Make Alias from the Menu bar

3 Once an alias has been created, it can then be moved to any location (in this case the Desktop)

Copying and Moving items

Items can be copied and moved within OS X by using the copy and paste method or by dragging:

Copy and paste

When an item is copied, it is placed on the Clipboard and remains there until another item is copied.

1 Select an item and select Edit>Copy from the Menu bar

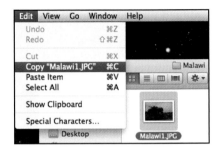

2 Move to the target location and select Edit>Paste Item from the Menu bar. The item is then pasted into the new location

Edit	View	Go	Window
Undo Rename			⌘Z
Redo			⇧⌘Z
Cut			⌘X
Copy			⌘C
Paste Item			**⌘V**
Select All			⌘A

Hold down the Option key while dragging to copy an item rather than moving it.

Dragging

Drag a file from one location into another to move it to that location

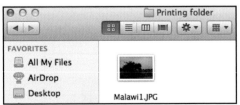

Working with Folders

When OS X is first installed, there are various folders that have already been created to hold programs and files. Some of these are essential (i.e. those containing programs) while others are created as an aid for where you might want to store the files that you create (such as the Pictures and Movies folders). Once you start working with OS X you will probably want to create your own folders, in which to store and organize your documents. This can be done on the desktop or within any level of your existing folder structure. To create a new folder:

1 Access the location in which you want to create the new folder (e.g. your Home folder) and select File>New Folder from the Menu bar

2 A new, empty, folder is inserted at the selected location (named "untitled folder")

Don't forget

Folders are always denoted by a folder icon. This is the same regardless of the Finder view which is selected. The only difference is that the icon is larger in Icon view than in List or Column views.

3 Overtype the file name with a new one. Press Enter

OS X Lion

Beware

You can create as many "nested" folders (i.e. folders within other folders) as you want. However, this makes your folder structure more complicated and, after time, you may forget where all your folders are and what they contain.

OS X Lion

4 Double-click on a folder to view its contents (at this point it should be empty)

Don't forget

Content can be added to an empty folder by dragging it from another folder and dropping it into the new one.

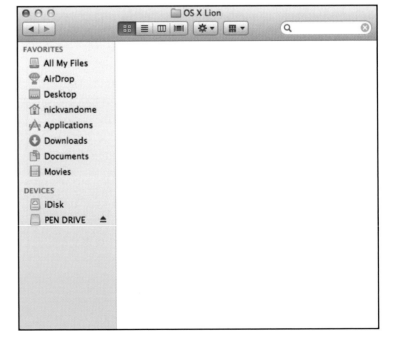

Smart Folders

When working on any computer it is inevitable that you will soon have a number of related files in different locations. This could be because you save your images in one folder, your word processing documents in another, web pages in another and so on. This can cause difficulties when you are trying to keep track of a lot of related documents. OS X overcomes this problem through the use of Smart Folders. These are folders that you set up using Finder search results as the foundation. Then when new items are created that meet the original criteria they are automatically included within the Smart Folder. To create a Smart Folder:

1 Conduct a search with the Finder search box

2 Once the search is completed, click the Save button to create a Smart Folder

3 Enter a name for the new Smart Folder and click Save

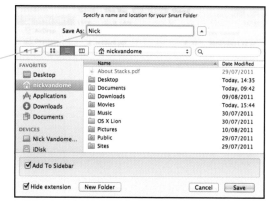

4 The Smart Folder is added to the Finder Sidebar. Click the Smart Folder to view its contents

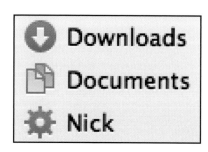

Hot tip

Numerous different Smart Folders can be created, for different types of files and information.

Don't forget

If you set a very precise criteria for a Smart Folder this will result in a fewer number of items being included within it.

Spring-loaded Folders

Another method for moving items with the Finder is to use the spring-loaded folder option. This enables you to drag items into a folder and then view the contents of the folder before you drop the item into it. This means that you can drag items into nested folders in a single operation. To do this:

Hot tip

The spring-loaded folder technique can be used to move items between different locations within the Finder, e.g. for moving files from your Pictures folder into your Home folder.

Beware

Do not release the mouse button until you have reached the location into which you want to place the selected item.

1 Select the item you want to move

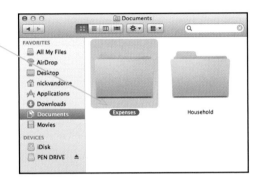

2 Drag the selected item over the folder into which you want to place it. Keep the mouse held down

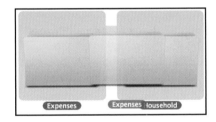

3 The folder will open, revealing its contents. The selected item can either be dropped into the folder or, if there are sub-folders, the same operation can be repeated until you find the folder into which you want to place the selected item

Burnable Folders

With the increasing use of images, digital video and music files, computer users are frequently copying data from their computers onto CDs. In some cases this can be a frustrating process but in OS X the use of burnable folders can make the process much quicker. These are folders that can be created specifically for the contents to be burned onto a CD or DVD. To do this:

1 In the Finder, select File>New Burn Folder from the Menu bar

Burn Folder

2 The burn folder is created in the Finder window which was active when Step 1 was performed. Click on the folder name and overtype to give it a unique name

3 Select the items that you want to burn and drag and drop or copy and paste them into the burn folder

4 Click here to burn the disk

Hot tip

Applications such as iTunes and iPhoto can be used to burn CDs using the content within that application, but burnable folders are the best way to combine files from a variety of different applications and then burn them onto disks.

Selecting Items

Programs and files within OS X folders can be selected by a variety of different methods:

Selecting by dragging
Drag the cursor to encompass the items to be selected. The selected items will become highlighted.

Selecting by clicking
Click once on an item to select it, hold down Shift and then click on another item in a list to select a consecutive group of items.

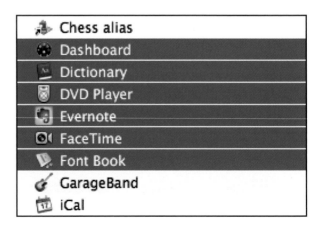

To select a non-consecutive group, select the first item by clicking on it once, then hold down the Command key (the one with the Apple symbol on it) and select the other required items. The selected items will appear highlighted.

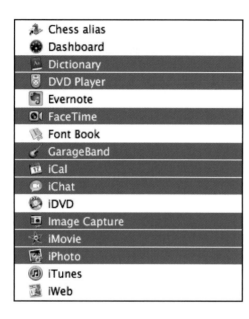

Select All

To select all of the items in a folder, select Edit>Select All from the Menu bar:

Actions Button

The Finder Actions Button provides a variety of options for any item, or items, selected in the Finder. To use this:

1   Select an item, or group of items, about which you want to find out additional information

2   Click on the Actions button on the Finder toolbar

Hot tip

If an image has been selected, the Actions button can be used to set it as the Desktop Picture, by selecting this option at the bottom of the Actions menu.

3   The available options for the selected item, or items, are displayed. These include Get Info, which displays additional information about an item, such as file type, file size, creation and modification dates and the default program for opening the item

Labelling Items

With the Actions Button it is possible to label items (including files, folders and programs) so that they can easily be identified for specific purposes. This could be for items that were created on a certain date or to quickly identify a particular type of document. To do this:

1 Select an item, or group of items, to which you want to apply labels

Don't forget

Labels are visible regardless of the View option that is selected in the Finder.

2 Click the Actions button

3 Select a color for the label, or labels

4 The colored labels are applied to the selected items. Other items can then have other label colors applied to them

Menus

The main Apple menu bar in OS X contains a variety of menus, which are consistent regardless of the program in operation:

- Apple menu. This is denoted by a translucent blue apple and contains general information about the computer, a preferences option for changing the functionality and appearance of the Dock and options for closing down the computer

- Finder menu. This contains preferences options for amending the functionality and appearance of the Finder and also options for emptying the Trash and accessing other programs (under the Services option)

- File menu. This contains common commands for working with open documents, such as opening and closing files, creating aliases, moving to the Trash, ejecting external devices and burning discs

- Edit menu. This contains common commands that apply to the majority of programs used on the Mac. These include undo, cut, copy, paste, select all and show the contents of the clipboard, i.e. items that have been cut or copied

- View. This contains options for how windows and folders are displayed within the Finder and for customizing the Finder toolbar

- Go. This can be used to navigate around your computer. This includes moving to your Home folder, your iDisk, your Applications folder, recently opened items and also remote servers for connecting to other computers on a network

- Window. This contains commands to organize the currently open programs and files on your desktop

- Help. This contains the Mac Help files which contain information about all aspects of OS X Lion

4 Navigating in Lion

OS X Lion introduces multi–touch gestures for navigating around your programs and documents. This chapter looks at how to use this to simplify getting around your Mac.

A New Way of Navigating

One of the most revolutionary features of Lion is the way in which you can navigate around your applications, web pages and documents. This involves a much greater reliance on swiping on a trackpad or adapted mouse: techniques that have been imported from the iPhone and the iPad. These are known as multi-touch gestures and to take full advantage of these you will need to have one of the following devices:

- A trackpad. This will be found on new MacBooks

- A Magic Trackpad. This can be used with an iMac, a Mac Mini or a Mac Pro. It works wirelessly via Bluetooth

- A Magic Mouse. This can be used with an iMac, a Mac Mini or a Mac Pro. It works wirelessly via Bluetooth

All of these devices work using a swiping technique with fingers moving over their surface. This should be done with a light touch; it is a gentle swipe, rather than any pressure being applied to the device.

The trackpads and Magic Mouse do not have any buttons in the same way as traditional devices. Instead specific areas are clickable so that you can still perform left and right click operations:

Don't forget

If you do not have a trackpad, a Magic Trackpad or a Magic Mouse you can still navigate within OS X Lion with a traditional mouse and the use of scroll bars in windows.

1 Click on the bottom left corner for traditional left-click operations

2 Ctrl+click on the bottom right corner for traditional right-click operations

Pointing and Clicking

A trackpad or Magic Mouse can be used to perform a variety of pointing and clicking tasks.

1 Tap with one finger in the middle of the trackpad or Magic Mouse to perform a single click operation i.e. to click on a button or click on an open window

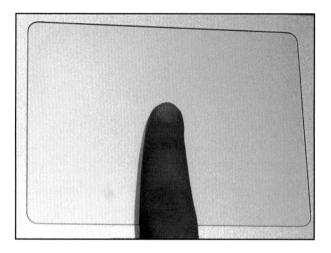

2 Tap with two fingers in the middle of the trackpad or Magic Mouse to access any contextual menus associated with an item (this is the equivalent of the traditional right-click with a mouse)

...cont'd

3 Highlight a word or phrase and double-tap with three fingers to see look-up information for the selected item. This is frequently a dictionary definition but it can also be a Wikipedia entry

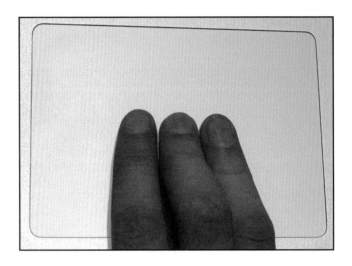

Beware

If you have too many functions set using the same number of fingers, some of them may not work. See page 82–84 for details about setting preferences for multi-gestures.

4 Move over an item and drag with three fingers to move the item around the screen

70

No More Scroll Bars

Another innovation in OS X Lion is the removal of scroll bars that are constantly visible on a web page or document. Instead, there are scroll bars that only appear when you are moving around a page or document. When you stop, the scroll bars melt away. Scrolling is done by multi-touch gestures on a trackpad or Magic Mouse and these gestures are looked at on the following pages. To perform scrolling with OS X Lion:

1 Scroll around a web page or document using the two finger multi-touch technique (see page 73). As you move up or down a page the scroll bar appears

Don't forget

Web pages and document windows can also be navigated around by dragging on the scroll bars using a mouse or a trackpad.

2 When you stop scrolling the bar disappears, to allow optimum viewing area for your web page or document

Scrolling and Zooming

One of the common operations on a computer is scrolling on a page, whether it is a web page or a document. Traditionally this has been done with a mouse and a cursor. However, using a trackpad or a Magic Mouse you can now do all of your scrolling with your fingers. There are a number of options for doing this:

Scrolling up and down

To move up and down web pages or documents, use two fingers on the trackpad and swipe up or down. The page moves in the opposite direction to the one in which you are swiping i.e. if you swipe up, the page moves down and vice versa:

72

① Open a web page

② Position two fingers in the middle of the trackpad

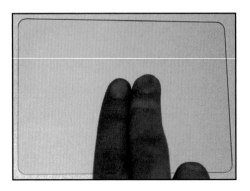

3 Swipe them up to move down the page

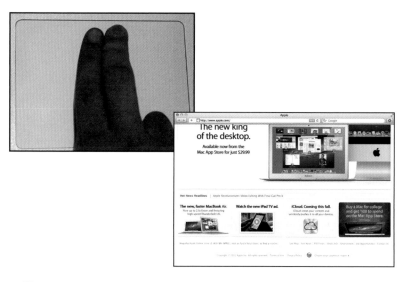

4 Swipe them down to move up a page

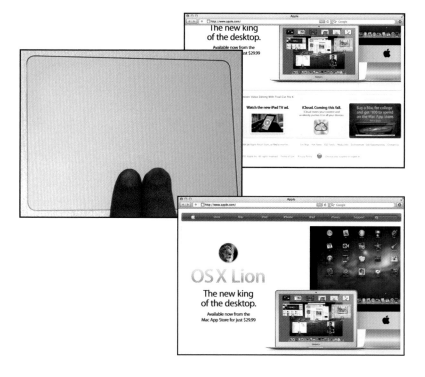

...cont'd

Zooming in and out

To zoom in or out on web pages or documents:

1 To zoom in, position your thumb and forefinger in the middle of the trackpad

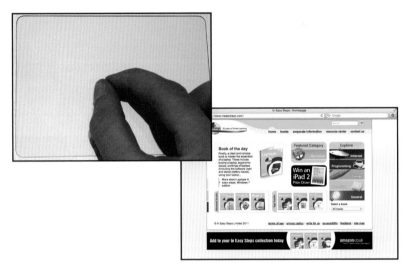

Hot tip

Pages can also be zoomed in on by double-clicking with two fingers.

74

2 Spread them outwards to zoom in on a web page or document

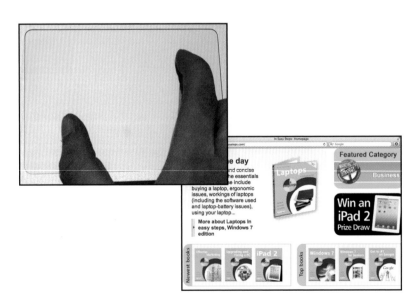

3 To zoom out, position your thumb and forefinger at opposite corners of the trackpad

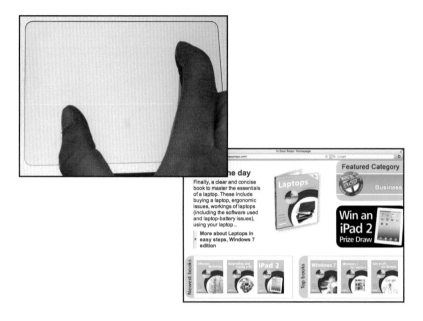

Don't forget

There is a limit on how far you can zoom in or out on a web page or document, to ensure that it does not distort the content too much.

4 Swipe them into the center of the trackpad to zoom in

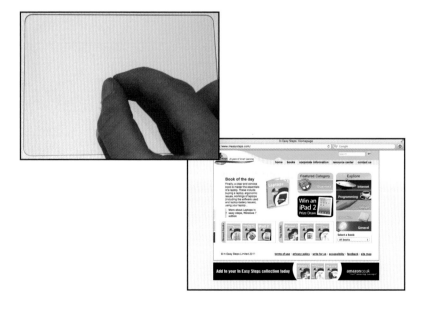

...cont'd

Moving between pages

With multi-touch gestures it is possible to swipe between pages within a document. To do this:

1 Position two fingers to the left or right of the trackpad

2 Swipe to the opposite side of the trackpad to move through the document

Moving between full-screen apps

In addition to moving between pages by swiping, it is also possible to move between different apps, when they are in full-screen mode. To do this:

Don't forget

See Chapter Five for details about using full-screen apps.

1 Position three fingers to the left or right of the trackpad

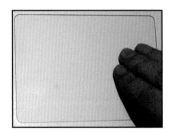

2 Swipe to the opposite side of the trackpad to move through the available full-screen apps

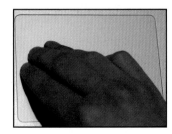

Showing the Desktop

To show the whole Desktop, regardless of how many files or apps are open:

① Position your thumb and three fingers in the middle of the trackpad

② Swipe to the opposite corners of the trackpad to display the Desktop

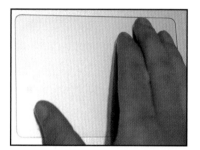

③ The Desktop is displayed, with all items minimized around the side of the screen

Mission Control

Mission Control is a function in OS X Lion that helps you organize all of your open apps, full-screen apps and documents. It also enables you to quickly view the Dashboard and Desktop. Within Mission Control there are also Spaces, where you can group together similar types of documents. To use Mission Control:

Don't forget

For more details about the Dashboard, see Chapter Six.

1 Click on this button on the Dock, or

2 Swipe upwards with three fingers on the trackpad or Magic Mouse

Don't forget

Click on a window in Mission Control to access it and exit the Mission Control window.

 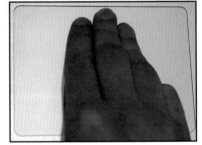

3 All open files and apps are visible via Mission Control

Don't forget

The top row of Mission Control contains the Dashboard, the Desktop and any full-screen apps.

4 If there is more than one window open for an app they will be grouped together by Mission Control

Safari

5 If an app is made full-screen it automatically appears along the top row

Safari   Preview

6 Desktop items are grouped together on the top row within Mission Control within an area called a Space (see following two pages)

Desktop

Spaces and Exposé

The top level of Mission Control contains Spaces, which are areas into which you can group certain apps, e.g. the iLife apps such as iPhoto and iTunes. This means that you can access these apps independently from every other open item. This helps organize your apps and files. To use Spaces:

1 Move the cursor over the top right-hand corner of Mission Control

2 A new Space is created along the top row of Mission Control

Don't forget

Preferences for Spaces and Exposé can be set within the Mission Control System Preference.

80

3 Drag an app onto the Space

Hot tip

Create different Spaces for different types of content e.g. one for productivity and one for entertainment.

4 Drag additional apps onto the Space

5 When you create additional Spaces the content of each Space is shown on its own when you access Mission Control

Exposé

Exposé is a function that enables you to view all of the open documents within an app. To use this:

1 Position three fingers at the top of the trackpad or Magic Mouse and swipe down, or press the F10 key (Fn+F10 on a laptop)

2 The open documents for the current app are displayed

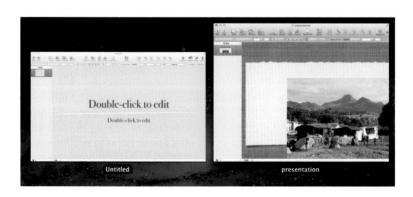

Multi-Touch Preferences

Some multi-touch gestures only have a single action, which cannot be changed. However, others have options for changing the action for a specific gesture. This is done within the Trackpad preferences, where a full list of multi-touch gestures is shown:

Point & Click Preferences

Hot tip

When setting multi-touch preferences try to avoid having too many gestures using the same number of fingers, in case some of them override the others.

1 Access the System Preferences and click on the Trackpad button

2 Click on the Point & Click tab

3 The actions are described on the left, with a graphic explanation on the right

4 If there is a down arrow next to an option, click on it to change the way an action is activated

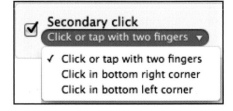

Scroll & Zoom Preferences

1 Click on the Scroll & Zoom tab   Scroll & Zoom

2 The actions are described on the left, with a graphic explanation on the right

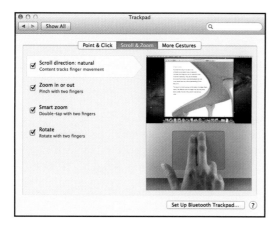

More Gestures Preferences

1 Click on the More Gestures tab   More Gestures

2 The actions are described on the left, with a graphic explanation on the right

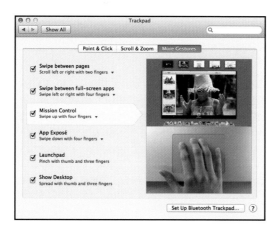

...cont'd

Multi-Touch Gestures

The full list of multi-touch gestures, with their default action are:

Point & Click

- Tap to click — tap with one finger
- Secondary click — click or tap with two fingers
- Look up — double-tap with three fingers
- Three finger drag — move with three fingers

Scroll & Zoom

- Scroll direction: natural — content tracks finger movement
- Zoom in or out — spread or pinch with two fingers
- Smart zoom — double-tap with two fingers
- Rotate — rotate with two fingers

More Gestures

- Swipe between pages — scroll left or right with two fingers
- Swipe between full-screen apps — swipe left or right with three fingers
- Access Mission Control — swipe up with three fingers
- App Exposé — swipe down with three fingers
- Access Launchpad — pinch with thumb and three fingers
- Show Desktop — spread with thumb and three fingers

5 OS X Lion Apps

Apps, or applications, are the programs with which you start putting Lion to use, either for work or for fun. This chapter looks at accessing your apps and obtaining more via the online Apple App Store.

Launchpad

Even though the Dock can be used to store shortcuts to your applications, it is limited in terms of space. The full set of applications on your Mac can be found in the Finder (see Chapter Three) but OS X Lion introduce a new feature that allows you to quickly access and manage all of your applications. These include the ones that are pre-installed on your Mac and also any that you install yourself or download from the Apple App Store. This feature is called Launchpad. To use it:

1 Click once on this button on the Dock

2 All of the apps (applications) are displayed

3 Similar types of apps can be grouped together in individual folders. By default, the Utilities are grouped in this way

4 To create a group of similar apps, drag the icon for one over another

5 The apps are grouped together in a folder and Launchpad gives it a name, based on the types of apps within the folder

6 To change the name, click on it once and overtype it with the new name

7 The folder appears within the Launchpad window

8 To remove an app, click and hold on it until it starts to jiggle and a cross appears. Click on the cross to remove it

Don't forget

System apps, i.e. the ones that already come with your Mac, cannot be removed in the Launchpad, only ones you have downloaded.

Full-Screen Apps

When working with apps we all like to be able to see as much of a window as possible. With OS X Lion this is now possible with the full-screen app. This allows you to expand an app with this functionality so that it takes up the whole of your monitor or screen with a minimum of toolbars visible. Some apps have this functionality but some do not. To use full-screen apps:

1 By default an app appears on the desktop with other window behind it

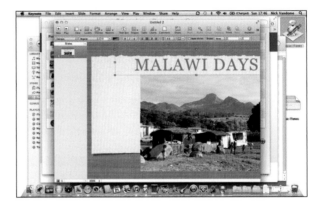

Don't forget

If the button in Step 2 is not visible then the app does not have the full-screen functionality.

2 Click on this button at the top right-hand corner of the app's window

3 The app is expanded to take up the whole window. The main Apple Menu bar and the Dock are hidden

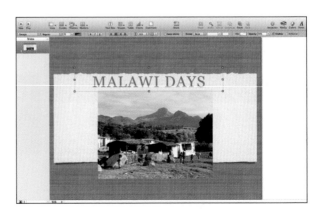

4   To view the
main Menu bar,
move the cursor
over the top of
the screen

5   You can move between all full-screen apps by swiping
with three fingers left or right on a trackpad or Magic
Mouse

Hot tip

For more information
about navigating with
multi-touch gestures see
Chapter Four.

6   Move the cursor over the top right-hand corner
of the screen and click on this button to close
the full-screen functionality

7   In Mission Control all of the open full-screen apps are
shown in the top row

OS X Applications

OS X Lion applications include:

- **Address Book.** (See Chapter Six)

- **Automator**. (See Chapter Ten)

- **Calculator.** A basic calculator

- **Chess**. Play online chess against your Mac computer

- **Dashboard**. (See Chapter Six)

- **Dictionary**. A digital dictionary

- **DVD Player.** Used to play and view DVDs

- **FaceTime.** Can be used for video calls (See Chapter Seven)

- **Font Book.** (See Chapter Six)

- **Front Row**. A program for accessing music, movies or photos with a remote control

- **iCal.** (See Chapter Six)

- **iChat.** (See Chapter Six)

- **Image Capture**. For downloading digital images

- **iPhoto, iTunes, iMovie, iDVD, iWeb and GarageBand.** (See Chapter Eight)

- **Mail**. The default email program

- **Mission Control.** The function for organizing your desktop

- **Photo Booth.** An app for creating photo effects

- **Preview.** (See Chapter Six)

- **QuickTime Player**. The default application for viewing video

- **Safari**. The OS X specific Web browser

- **Stickies**. A small program for adding note-like reminders

- **TextEdit**. A program for editing text files

- **Time Machine**. OS X's backup facility

Accessing the App Store

The App Store is another OS X app. This is an online facility where you can download and buy new apps. These cover a range of categories such as productivity, business and entertainment. When you select or buy an app from the App Store, it is downloaded automatically by Launchpad and appears here next to the rest of the apps.

To buy apps from the App Store you need to have an Apple ID and account. If you have not already set this up, it can be done when you first access the App Store. To use the App Store:

Don't forget

The App Store is an online function so you will need an Internet connection with which to access it.

1 Click on this icon on the Dock or within the Launchpad

2 The homepage of the App Store contains the current top featured apps

Hot tip

You can set up an Apple ID when you first set up your Mac or you can do it when you register for the App Store or the iTunes Store.

3 Your account information and quick link categories are listed at the right-hand side of the page

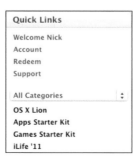

Downloading Apps

The App Store contains a wide range of apps: from small, fun apps, to powerful productivity ones. However, downloading them from the App Store is the same regardless of the type of app. The only differences are whether they require to be paid for or not and the length of time they take to download. To download an app from the App Store:

Browse through the App Store until you find the required app

Click on the app to view a detailed description about it

Click on the button underneath the app icon to download it. If there is no charge for the app the button will say Free

4 If there is a charge for the app, the button will say Buy App

5 Click on the Install App button

6 Enter your Apple ID account details to continue downloading the app

Sign in to download from the App Store.

If you have an Apple ID, sign in with it here. If you have used the iTunes Store or MobileMe, for example, you have an Apple ID. If you don't have an Apple ID, click Create Apple ID.

Apple ID	Password	Forgot?
nickvandome@mac.com		

(?) | Create Apple ID | | Cancel | Sign In |

7 The progress of the download is displayed in a progress bar underneath the Launchpad icon on the Dock

8 Once it has been downloaded, the app is available within Launchpad

TextEdit

Time Machine

Pages

SoundCloud

Don't forget

Depending on their size, different apps take differing amounts of time to be downloaded.

Don't forget

As you download more apps, additional pages will be created within the Launchpad to accommodate them.

Finding Apps

There are thousands of apps in the App Store and sometimes the hardest task is locating the ones you want. However, there are a number of ways in which finding apps is made as easy as possible.

1 Click on the Featured button

2 The main window has a range of categories such as New, What's Hot and Staff Favorites. At the right-hand side there is a panel with a Top Ten Paid For apps

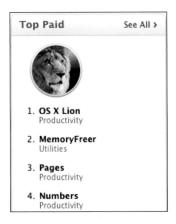

Hot tip

Another way to find apps is to type a keyword into the Search box at the top right-hand corner of the App Store window.

3 Underneath this is a list of the Top Ten Free apps

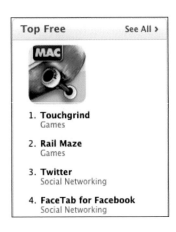

④ Click on the Top Charts button

⑤ The top apps for different categories are displayed

⑥ Click on the Categories button

⑦ Browse through the apps by specific categories, such as Business, Entertainment and Finance

Managing Your Apps

Once you have bought apps from the App Store you can view details of ones you have purchased and also install updated versions of them.

Purchased Apps

To view your purchased apps:

1 Click on the Purchased button

2 Details of you purchased apps are displayed (including those that are free)

Don't forget

Even if you interrupt a download and turn off your Mac you will still be able to resume the download when you restart your computer.

3 If a download of an app has been interrupted, click on the Resume button to continue with it

Updating Apps

Improvements and fixes are being developed constantly and these can be downloaded to ensure that all of your apps are up to date.

 When updates are available this is indicated by a red circle on the App Store icon in the Dock, in the same way as you would be alerted to new emails

Click on the Updates button

Full Deck Solitaire	– true Mac OS X Lion full screen mode
GRL Games	– stack dropping bug fix
Version 1.35	
Released 09 August 2011	

Information about the updates is displayed next to the app that is due to be updated

Click on the Update button to update an individual app   **UPDATE**

Click on the Update All button to update all of the apps that are due to be updated   **UPDATE ALL**

97

Sharing Apps

If you have more than one Mac computer you do not have to buy apps separately for each one. If you have purchased an app for one Mac you can also install it on other Macs without having to pay for it again. To do this:

1 Access the App Store and click on the Purchased button

2 Any apps that have been purchased on another Mac are displayed in the Purchased window

Purchases		Purchase Date
Keynote Apple®		17 August 2011
SoundCloud SoundCloud Ltd.		17 August 2011
Plane Control Lite Istom Games Kft.		03 August 2011
Full Deck Solitaire GRL Games		03 August 2011
Pages Apple®		31 July 2011
Evernote Evernote		30 July 2011

3 Click on the Install button to install an app on a Mac that does not yet have it

4 To install the app you will need to enter your Apple ID, although you will not be charged for the app

Sign in to download from the App Store.
If you have an Apple ID, sign in with it here. If you have used the iTunes Store or MobileMe, for example, you have an Apple ID. If you don't have an Apple ID, click Create Apple ID.

Apple ID
nickvandome@mac.com

Password   Forgot?
••••••

? | Create Apple ID | Cancel | Sign In

6 Getting Productive

There are several apps within OS X Lion that can be used to create, store and display information. This chapter shows how to access and use these programs, so that you can get the most out of Lion as an efficient and productive work tool.

Dashboard

The OS X Dashboard is a collection of widgets within OS X that can be used for common tasks such as a calendar, an address book and a dictionary. To use the Dashboard:

1 Click once on this icon on the Dock

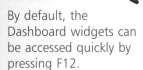

2 The Dashboard widgets are maximized on the screen and superimposed over the rest of the active programs

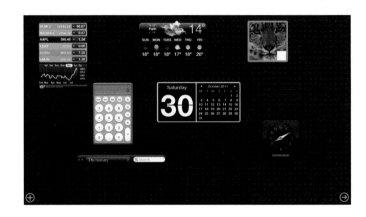

3 Click here to view the panel of all of the available widgets (by default, only a selection are visible when the Dashboard is accessed)

4 The full range of widgets are shown here

5 To make a widget active, drag it from the Dashboard panel onto the main window

Adding Dashboard Widgets

In order to maximize the benefit of the Dashboard, Apple have encouraged developers to create and publish their own widgets. This has resulted in dozens of new widgets that can be downloaded from the Apple website at www.apple.com/downloads/dashboard/. From here, the available widgets can be viewed and downloaded:

1 Click here to download specific widgets

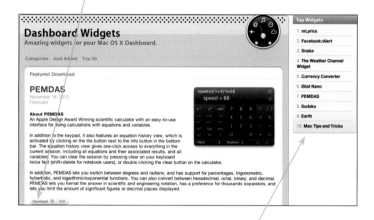

2 Click here to view the top downloads

3 Scroll down the downloads page and click here to view available widgets by category

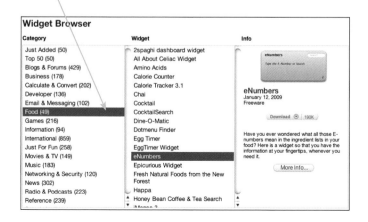

Spotlight Search

Spotlight is the dedicated search program for OS X. It can be used over the files on your Mac. To use Spotlight:

Beware

Spotlight starts searching for items as soon as you start typing a word. So don't worry if some of the first results look inappropriate as these will disappear once you have finished typing the full word.

1 Click on this icon at the far right of the Apple Menu bar

2 In the Spotlight box, enter the search keyword(s)

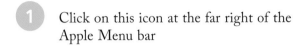

3 The results are displayed according to type

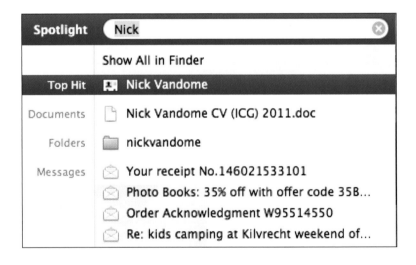

4   Click on an item to view it or see its contents (in the case of folders)

5   If you select a folder, it will be displayed in its location within the Finder

6   Options are also available for searching the Web or Wikipedia for the search keyword(s)

7   Click on the Spotlight Preferences... link to specify the order, by category, in which results appear

Spotlight Preferences...

Address Book

The Address Book can be used to store contact information, which can then be used in different applications and even published on the Web so that you can access it from computers around the world.

Overview

The Address Book contains contact information, either for groups or for individuals. The Address Book can display this information in two ways:

1 Click here to view card and column information

2 Click here to view card information only i.e. individual Address Book entries

Adding contact information

The main function of the Address Book is to include details of personal and business contacts. This has to be done manually for each entry, but it can prove to be a valuable resource once it has been completed. To add contact information:

1 Click here to edit contact information

2 Click on a category and enter contact information. Press Tab to move to the next field

Hot tip

Address Book can import contacts in the vCard format (which uses the .vcf extension). So if you have a lot of contacts on a Windows-based PC you can export them as vCards, copy them onto a disk and import them into Address Book. To do this, select File>Import>vCards from the Menu bar and browse to the folder on the disk on which they are held.

3 Click here and browse your hard drive to add a photograph for the selected contact

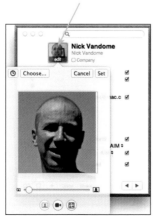

...cont'd

Creating groups

In addition to creating individual entries in the Address Book, group contacts can also be created. This is a way of grouping contacts with similar interests. Once a group has been created, all of the entries within it can be accessed and contacted by selecting the relevant entry under the Group column. To create a group:

1 Click on this button under the Group panel to create a new group entry

2 Give the new group a name

> Work

3 Drag individual entries into the group (the individual entries are retained too)

All Contacts

4 Click on a group name to view the members of the group

iCal

Electronic calendars are now a standard part of modern life and with OS X this function is performed by the iCal program. Not only can this be used on your Mac, it can also be synchronized with other Apple devices such as an iPod or an iPhone. To create a calendar:

1. Click on this icon on the Dock, or in the Launchpad

2. Select whether to view the calendar by day, week or month

Hot tip

When iCal is opened it displays the current date in the icon on the Dock.

3. Click on the Today button to view the current day. Click on the forward or back arrows to move to the next day, week, month or year, depending on what is selected in Step 2

Hot tip

Swipe with two fingers to the left or right on a trackpad or a Magic Mouse to move between days, weeks, months or years within iCal.

107

...cont'd

Adding Events

To add new events:

1   Select a date and double click on it, or Ctrl+click on the date

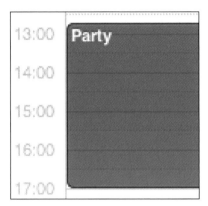

2   Select New Event

3   Enter the details for the new event

4   Double-click on an item and select options for how it is displayed

Adding a Quick Event

To add a Quick Event for a selected day:

1 Click on this button on the top of the iCal window

2 Enter the name of the event in the Create Quick Event box

3 The same options as in Step 4 on the previous page are shown

Publishing a calendar

If you have a MobileMe account you can publish calendars to it so that you can always access this information online. To do this:

1 Select Calendar>Publish from the iCal Menu bar

2 Select options for how you would like to publish the calendar and click on the Publish button

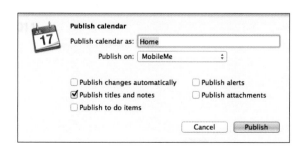

Don't forget

In fall/autumn 2011 the MobileMe facility will be replaced by iCloud, although it will still be available until 2012.

Font Book

The Font Book is an app that can be used to add, organize and remove fonts within OS X. To use the Font Book:

Viewing fonts

The available fonts on the system can be viewed via the Font Book:

Click on a Collection and a Font. An example is displayed here

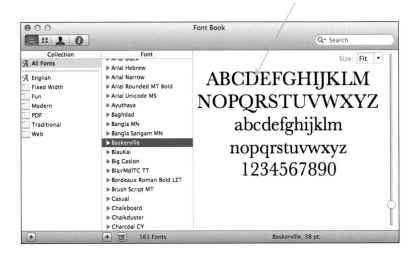

Adding fonts

New fonts can be added through Font Book and existing fonts can be disabled throughout your computer. To do this:

1 Click here to add a new font

2 Click here to disable an existing font

Preview

Preview is an OS X app that can be used to view multiple file types, particularly image file formats. This can be useful if you just want to view documents without editing them in a dedicated program, such as an image editing program. Preview can also be used to view PDF (Portable Document Format) files and also preview documents before they are printed. To use Preview:

1 Double-click on an item within the Finder

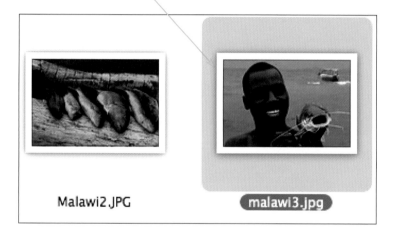

Malawi2.JPG   malawi3.jpg

2 The selected file is displayed by Preview

Don't forget

To open the Preview, click on this icon on the Dock or in the Launchpad:

111

Hot tip

If you want to edit digital images use either iPhoto or an image editing program such as Photoshop Elements from Adobe.

OS X Utilities

In addition to the programs in the Applications folder, there are also a number of utility programs that perform a variety of tasks within OS X. To access the Utilities:

 1 Open the Applications folder and double-click on the Utilities folder

2 The available utilities are displayed within the Utilities folder

- **Activity Monitor**. This contains information about the system memory being used and disk activity (see Chapter Ten for more details)

- **AirPort Utility**. This sets up the AirPort wireless networking facility

- **AppleScript Editor**. This can be used to create your own scripts with Apple's dedicated scripting program, AppleScript

- **Audio MIDI Setup**. This can be used for adding audio devices and setting their properties

- **Bluetooth File Exchange**. This determines how files are exchanged between your computer and other Bluetooth devices (if this function is enabled)

- **Boot Camp Assistant**. This can be used to run Windows operating systems on your Mac

- **ColorSync Utility**. This can be used to view and create color profiles on your computer. These can then be used by programs to try and match output color with the color that is displayed on the monitor

- **Console**. This displays the behind-the-scenes messages that are being passed around the computer while its usual tasks are being performed

- **DigitalColor Meter**. This can be used to measure the exact color values of a particular color

- **Disk Utility**. This can be used to view information about attached disks and repair errors

- **Grab**. This is a utility which can be used to capture screen shots. These are images of the screen at a given point in time. You can grab different portions of the screen and even menus. The resultant images can be saved into different file formats

- **Grapher**. This is a utility for creating simple or more complex scientific graphs

Don't forget

You may never need to use a utility like the Console, but it is worth having a look at it just to see the inner workings of a computer.

Hot tip

The Grab utility is invaluable if you are producing manuals or books and need to display examples of a screen or program.

113

...cont'd

- **Java Preferences**. This is a folder that contains utilities that can be used to run and work with Java programs. It has specific utilities for Input Method Hotkey, Java Preferences and Java Web Start

- **Keychain Access**. This deals with items such as passwords when they are needed for networking. These do not have to be set but it can save time if you have to enter passwords on a lot of occasions. It also ensures that there is greater security for items protected by passwords

- **Migration Assistant**. This helps in the transfer of files between two Mac computers. This can be used if you buy a new Mac and you need to transfer files from another one

- **Network Utility**. This is a problem determination guide to see if the problem is on the workstation or the network

- **Podcast Capture**. This enables you to record audio and video on your Mac and then output it to an online podcast provider

- **System Information**. This contains details of the hardware devices and software applications that are installed on your computer (see Chapter Ten for more details)

- **Terminal**. This is used as an entry point into the world of UNIX. Within the Terminal you can view the workings of UNIX and also start to write your own programs, if you have some UNIX programming knowledge

- **VoiceOver Utility**. This has various options for how the VoiceOver function works within OS X. This is the digital voice that can be used to read out what is on the screen and it is particularly useful for users who are visually impaired

Printing

OS X Lion makes the printing process as simple as possible, partly by being able to automatically install new printers as soon as they are connected to your Mac. However, it is also possible to install printers manually. To do this:

1 Open the System Preferences folder and click on the Print & Scan button

2 Currently installed printers are displayed in the Printers List. Click here to add a new printer and click on either the Add Other Printer or Scanner link or any currently available printers

3 OS X Lion loads the required printer driver (if it does not have a specific one it will try and use a generic one)

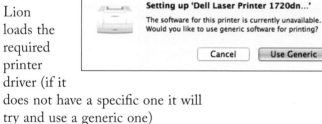

4 The details about the printer are available in the Print & Scan window

5 Once a printer has been installed documents can be printed by selecting File>Print from the Menu bar. Print settings can be set at this point and they can also be set by selecting File>Page/Print Setup from the Menu bar in most programs

Don't forget

For most printers, OS X will detect them when they are first connected and they should be ready to use immediately without the need to install any software or apply new settings.

Creating PDF Documents

PDF (Portable Document Format) is a file format that preserves the formatting of the original document and it can be viewed on a variety of computer platforms including Mac, Windows and UNIX. OS X has a built-in PDF function that can produce PDF files from most programs. To do this:

1 Open a file in any program and select File>Print from the Menu bar. Click on the PDF button and click on Save as PDF

2 Browse to a destination for the file and click Save

3 Look in the selected location to view the newly created PDF file

7 Internet and Email

This chapter shows how to get the most out of the Internet and email. It covers connecting to the Internet and how to use the OS X Web browser, Safari and its email program, Mail. It also covers text and video chatting and the use of RSS news feeds.

Getting Connected

Access to the Internet is an accepted part of the computing world and it is unusual for users not to want to do this. Not only does this provide a gateway to the World Wide Web but also email.

Connecting to the Internet with a Mac is done through the System Preferences. To do this:

1. Click on the System Preferences icon on the Dock

2. Click on the Network icon

3. Check that your method of connecting to the Internet is active, i.e. colored green

4. Click on the Assist me... button to access wizards for connecting to the Internet with your preferred method of connection

5 Click on the Assistant... button

6 The Network Setup Assistant is used to configure your system so that you can connect to the Internet

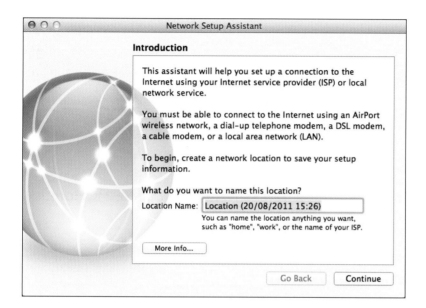

7 Enter a name for your connection

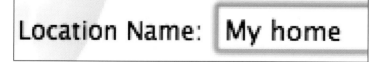

8 Click on the Continue button

...cont'd

9 Select an option for how you will connect to the Internet, e.g. wireless, cable or telephone modem

10 Click on the Continue button   Continue

11 For a wireless connection, select an available wireless network. This will be the router that is being used to make the connection

Select the wireless network you want to join:

CRAIGIE1

juicyanno

NETGEAR

12 Enter a password for the router (this will have been created when you connected and configured the router)

Password: Selected network requires a password

••••••••

13 Click on the Continue button   Continue

14 The Ready to Connect window informs you that you are about to attempt to connect to your network

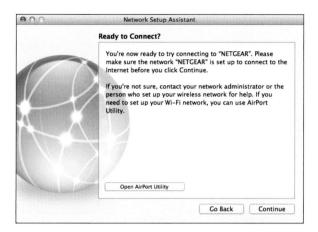

15 Click on the Continue button

16 You are informed if the connection has been successful

17 Click on the Done button

Safari

Safari is a Web browser that is designed specifically to be used with OS X. It is similar in most respects to other browsers, but it usually functions more quickly and works seamlessly with OS X.

Safari overview

 Click here on the Dock to launch Safari

Hot tip

If the Address Bar is not visible, select View from the Menu bar and check on the Address Bar option. From this menu you can also select or deselect items such as the Back/Forward buttons and the Stop/Reload buttons.

Back and forward   Address bar   Refresh   Search

Bookmarks bar

Page content

 Select Safari> Preferences from the Menu bar to specify settings for the way Safari operates and displays Web pages

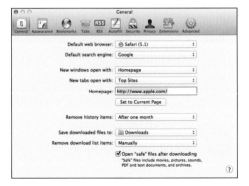

Adding bookmarks

Bookmarks are a device by which you can create quick links to your favorite Web pages or the ones you visit most frequently. Bookmarks can be added to a menu or the Bookmarks bar in Safari which makes them even quicker to access. Folders can also be created to store the less frequently used bookmarks. To view and create bookmarks:

1. Click here to view all bookmarks

2. All of the saved bookmarks can be accessed from the Collections window and viewed in the main window. Click on a page to move to it

3. Click here to create a bookmark for the page currently being viewed

4. Enter a name for the bookmark and select a location in which to store it

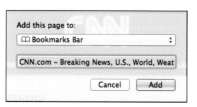

5. Click on the Add button

Beware

Only keep your most frequently used bookmarks in the Bookmarks Bar. Otherwise some of them will cease to be visible, as there will be too many entries for the available space.

123

Don't forget

Safari is a full-screen app and can be expanded by clicking the double arrow in the top right corner. For more information on full-screen apps, see Chapter Five.

Safari Top Sites

Within Safari there is a facility to view a graphical representation of the websites that you visit most frequently. This can be done from a button on the Safari Menu bar. To do this:

1 Click on this button to view the Top Sites window

2 The Top Sites window contains thumbnails of the websites that you have visited most frequently with Safari

3 Click on the Edit button to change the properties of the Top Sites thumbnails

4 Click on the cross to delete a thumbnail from the Top Sites window. Click on the pin to keep it there permanently

5 Click on a thumbnail to go to the full site

6 Use these buttons to select the size of the thumbnails

7 When you open a new tab the first window will be the Top Sites

Don't forget

The Top Sites window is also accessed if you open a new window within Safari.

8 To add a new site to the Top Sites, open another window and drag the URL (website address) into the Top Sites

Safari Reader

Web pages can be complex and cluttered things at times. On occasions you may want to just read the content of one story on a web pages without all of the extra material in view. In Safari this can be done with the Reader function. To do this:

Beware

Not all web pages support the Reader functionality in Safari.

1 Select View>Show Reader from the Safari menu bar

View	History	Bookm

Hide Toolbar
Customize Toolbar...

Hide Bookmarks Bar
Show Tab Bar
Show Status Bar

Show Reader

2 Click on the Reader button in the address bar of a web page that supports this functionality

3 The button turns purple once the Reader is activated

4 The content is displayed in a text format, with any photos from the original

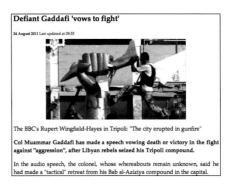

Defiant Gaddafi 'vows to fight'

24 August 2011 Last updated at 09:33

The BBC's Rupert Wingfield-Hayes in Tripoli: "The city erupted in gunfire"

Col Muammar Gaddafi has made a speech vowing death or victory in the fight against "aggression", after Libyan rebels seized his Tripoli compound.

In the audio speech, the colonel, whose whereabouts remain unknown, said he had made a "tactical" retreat from his Bab al-Aziziya compound in the capital.

5 Click on this button on the Safari toolbar if you want to save a page to read at a later date

6 Click on this button to add the page

Add Page

Safari RSS

RSS, which stands for Really Simple Syndication, is a method of producing regularly updated information on websites. It works by using XML (Extensible Markup Language) and is most frequently seen on news websites: the RSS feed displays the latest news. In order for an RSS feed to be viewed, the browser has to support the RSS technology. Safari does this and when it comes across a website with RSS this icon is displayed in the Safari address bar:

Once an RSS enabled site has been located the news feeds can be accessed by clicking on the RSS icon. To access RSS feeds:

Don't forget

RSS is becoming increasingly popular and more and more websites are now using it for areas such as news.

1 Click here to access RSS feeds for a site that has this facility available

2 Specific settings can be made in the RSS window

Mail

Email is an essential element for most computer users and Macs come with their own email program called Mail. This covers all of the email functionality that anyone could need.

When first using Mail you have to set up your email account. This information will be available from the company who provides your email service, although in some cases Mail may obtain this information automatically. To view your Mail account details:

Don't forget

Mail is a full-screen app and can be expanded by clicking the double arrow in the top right corner. For more information on full-screen apps, see Chapter Five.

128

Don't forget

If you are setting up a new email account you will need to get the details to enter from your Internet Service Provider (ISP).

Don't forget

Mail can download messages from all of the accounts that you have set up within the Accounts preference.

1. Click on this icon on the Dock

2. Select Mail>Preferences from the Menu bar

3. Click on the Accounts tab

4. If it has not already been included, enter the details of your email account in the Account Information section

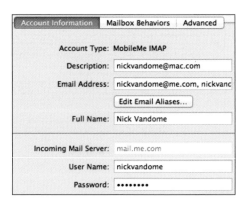

5. Click on this button to add a new email account

Using Email

Mail enables you to send and receive emails and also format them to your own style. This can be simply formatting text or adding customized stationery. To use Mail:

1 Click on the Get Mail button to download available email messages

2 Click on the New Message button to create a new email

3 Enter a recipient in the To box, a title in the Subject box and then text for the email in the main window

4 Click on the Format button to access options for formatting the text in the email

5 Click on these buttons to Reply to, Reply to All or Forward an email you have received

6 Select or open an email and click on the Delete button to remove it

129

Hot tip

To show the text underneath an icon in Mail, Ctrl+click next to an icon and select Icon & Text from the menu.

Hot tip

When entering the name of a recipient for a message, Mail will display details of matching names from your Address Book. For instance, if you type DA, all of the entries in your Address Book beginning with this will be displayed and you can select the required one.

Hot tip

If you Forward an email with an attachment then the attachment is included. If you Reply to an email the attachment will not be included.

...cont'd

Hot tip

It is worth occasionally checking in your Junk Mailbox, in case something you want has been put there.

Beware

Do not send files that are too large in terms of file size, otherwise the recipient may find it takes too long to download.

7 Click on the Junk button to mark an email as junk or spam. This trains Mail to identify junk mail. After a period of time, these types of messages will automatically be moved straight into the Junk mailbox

8 Click on the Attach button to browse your folders to include another file in your email. This can be items such as photos, word documents or pdf files

9 Click on the Photo Browser button to browse photos to add to an email

10 Click on the Show Stationery button to access a variety of templated designs that can added to your email

11 Select a Stationery design to add it to the email. Elements such as the text and photos can then be edited

Email Conversations

Within Mail you can view conversations i.e. groups of emails on the same subject. There is also a facility for showing your own replies within a conversation. To view a conversation:

Select View>Organize by Conversation from the Mail menu bar

Emails with the same subject are grouped together as a conversation in the left-hand pane. The number of grouped emails is show at the right-hand side

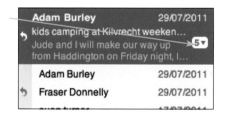

Click here to view the full list of emails

The full conversation is show in the right-hand pane

Click on this button to include your own messages in a conversation

Show Related Messages

Click on this button to hide your own messages in a conversation

Hide Related Messages

Adding Mailboxes

When you are dealing with email it is a good idea to create a folder structure (mailboxes) for your messages. This will allow you to sort your emails into relevant subjects when you receive them, rather than having all of them sitting in your Inbox. To add a structure of new mailboxes

1 Click on this button to view your current mailboxes

2 Click on the plus button at the bottom left-hand corner of the Mail window and select New Mailbox

3 Enter a name for the Mailbox and a location for where you would like it to be stored (by default this will be On My Mac)

4 The new mailbox is added to the current list

iChat

One issue with email is that you can never be sure when the recipient receives the message, or when they will reply to it. For a more immediate form of communication, instant messaging or video messaging can be used. This is done with the iChat program. To use this:

1 Click on this icon on the Dock

2 In order to chat to someone you have to add them as a buddy. To do this, click on the plus sign button and click on the Add Buddy link

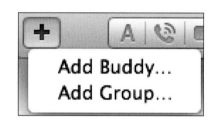

3 Enter the required details in the buddy window and click on the Add button

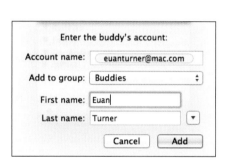

4 Select a buddy in the iChat window to make a call

5 Click on this button to make a video call

133

FaceTime

FaceTime is an app that has previously been used on the iPhone and iPod touch to make video calls to other compatible devices. However, this is now available with OS X Lion so that you can make and receive video calls from your Mac via iPhone, iPad and iPod Touches. To do this:

1 Click on this icon on the Dock

2 You require an Apple ID to use FaceTime. Enter your details or click on the Create New Account button

Enter Apple ID

Sign in with your Apple ID or create a new account to activate FaceTime.

nickvandome@mac.com

••••••••

Sign In

Create New Account

3 Once you have logged in you can make video calls by selecting people from your address book, or adding their phone number, providing they have a device that supports FaceTime

8 Digital Lifestyle

Leisure time, and how we use it, is a significant issue for everyone. Within the OS X environment there are several apps that can be used to create and manage your digital lifestyle. Some of these are known as the iLife suite of programs and cover photos, music, home movies, DVD creation, creating websites and composing music.

iPhoto

iPhoto is the photo management program for OS X. The intention of iPhoto is to make the organizing, manipulation and sharing of digital images as easy as possible. To begin using iPhoto and downloading photos:

1 Click once on this icon on the Dock

2 Connect your digital camera, or card reader, to your Mac via either USB or Firewire. The images on the connected device are displayed in the main iPhoto window

3 Click on the Import All... button to import all of the images from the camera, or card reader

Import All...

4 Select specific images and click on the Import Selected button

Import Selected

Once photographs have been downloaded by iPhoto they are displayed within the Library. This is the main storage area for all of the photographs that are added to iPhoto.

Viewing Photos

There are a variety of ways in which photos can be viewed and displayed in iPhoto:

1 In the main window double-click on an image

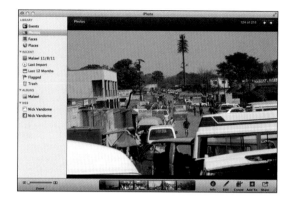

2 This displays it at full size (click on it once to return to the main window)

Hot tip

Zooming right in on a photo is an excellent way to view fine detail and see if the photo is properly in focus.

137

3 In the main window drag this slider to display images in the main iPhoto window at different sizes

Organizing Photos

Within iPhoto you can create albums to store different types of photos. To do this:

1 Select photos within the iPhoto window and click on the Add To button at the bottom right-corner of the main window

2 Click on the Album button

3 Click on the New Album button

4 Enter a name for the Album

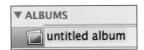

Don't forget

Once photos have been added to an album they are still visible in the main Library. The items in each album are just a reference back to the Library items.

5 The new album is included under the Albums section in the left-hand panel

6 To add photos to an album, drag them over the album name from the main iPhoto window

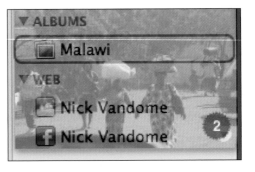

Editing and Sharing Photos

As well as using iPhoto for viewing and organizing photos there are also facilities for editing and sharing them:

 Click on this button to access the editing options

 Click on the Quick Fixes tab for options to quickly edit various aspects of a photo, such as rotating it, color editing techniques and cropping

 Click on the Effects tab to access various special effects that can be applied to a photo

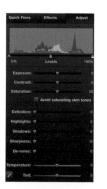 Click on the Adjust tab to access a range of more sophisticated color editing options

 Click on the Share button to access options for sharing your photos to photo sharing sites and also popular social networking sites

Beware

Most photos will benefit from some degree of editing but be careful not to overdo it, particularly with color editing and adjustments.

iTunes

Music is one of the areas that has revived Apple's fortunes in recent years, primarily through the iPod music player and iTunes, and also the iTunes music store, where music can be bought online. iTunes is a versatile program but its basic function is to play a music CD. To do this:

1 Click on this button on the Dock and insert the CD in the CD/DVD drive

2 By default, iTunes will open and display this window. Click No if you just want to play the CD

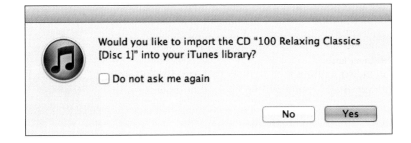

Would you like to import the CD "100 Relaxing Classics [Disc 1]" into your iTunes library?

☐ Do not ask me again

No   Yes

Beware

Never import music and use it for commercial purposes as this would be a breach of copyright.

3 Click on the CD name

DEVICES

100 Relaxing Classics... ⏏

4 Click on this button to play the whole CD

5 Click on the Import CD button if you want to copy (burn) the music from the CD onto your hard drive

Import CD

Managing Your Music

iTunes has a variety of ways to display and manage your music:

 Click on the Music link to see all of the music items within iTunes

 Click on this button to view the details of your music

✓	Name	Time	Artist	▲	Album
✓	Digital Booklet – The Suburbs ▣		Arcade Fire		The Suburbs
✓	The Suburbs	5:15	Arcade Fire		The Suburbs
✓	Ready to Start	4:16	Arcade Fire		The Suburbs
✓	Modern Man	4:40	Arcade Fire		The Suburbs
✓	Rococo	3:57	Arcade Fire		The Suburbs
✓	Empty Room	2:52	Arcade Fire		The Suburbs
✓	City With No Children	3:12	Arcade Fire		The Suburbs
✓	Half Light I	4:14	Arcade Fire		The Suburbs

Click on this button to view the cover view of your music. Swipe with two fingers on the trackpad to move between the covers or use the scroll bar below the covers

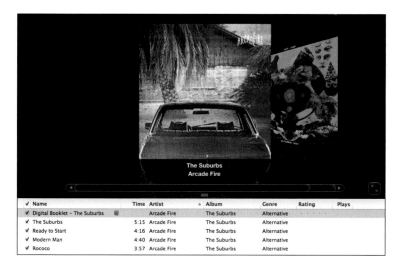

Purchasing Music

As well as copying music from CDs into iTunes, it is also possible to download a vast selection of music from the iTunes online store. To do this:

1 Click on the iTunes Store link to access the online store

2 Navigate around the iTunes store using the tabs along the top of the iTunes window

3 To find a specific item, enter the details in the Search box at the top right-hand corner of the iTunes window

4 Details of the item are displayed within the Store

5 Click on the Buy Album button to purchase the item.

Adding an iPod

Since their introduction in 2001 iPods have become an inescapable part of modern life. It is impossible to sit on a bus or a train without seeing someone with the ubiquitous white earbuds, humming away to their favorite tunes. iPods are for everyone and they are designed to work seamlessly with iTunes and the latter can be used to load music onto the former. To do this:

① Connect your iPod to the Mac with the supplied USB or Firewire cable

② iTunes will open automatically and display details about the attached iPod

Don't forget

iPods come in a variety of styles, colors, sizes and disk capacity.

143

③ iTunes should automatically start copying music from  the iTunes Library onto the iPod. If not, select the iPod under the Devices heading

④ Select File>Sync from the iTunes Menu bar or click on the Sync button to synchronize iTunes and your iPod

Sync

iMovie

For home movie buffs, iMovie offers options for downloading, creating, editing and publishing your efforts:

1 Click on this button on the Dock

2 Attach a digital video camera to your Mac with a Firewire cable

3 Click here to access the camera

4 Click here to select a camera for downloading or use the built-in FaceTime one to record your own movie

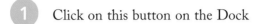

144

5 Click on the Capture... button to copy the video into iMovie

6 Click on the Done button to return to the editing environment

7 Downloaded video clips are shown here

8 Drag a clip into the project window to add it to a new video project

9 Use these buttons to add music, photos, text, transitions and maps to the project

iDVD

Once video has been created, it can be shared amongst family and friends on a DVD. This can be done through the iDVD program. To do this:

1. Click on this icon on the Dock

2. Click on the Create a New Project option

3. Give the project a name

Don't forget

All of your photos in iPhoto and music in iTunes are available to include in the DVD, through the audio and photos tabs.

4. Click on the Create button

5. Click on the Themes button

6. Click on the Media button to add Audio, Photos and Movies to your iDVD project

7. Click on this button to burn the iDVD project to a DVD

iWeb

It seems as if everybody has their own websites these days. Not only are they a great way to publish family information, they are also ideal for clubs or charity organizations. With the online .Mac service and a program called iWeb it is possible to quickly get up and running on the Web with your own site. To do this:

1 Click on this icon on the Dock

2 Select a template for the design of your website

3 Click on these buttons to add a theme, text and shapes to your page

4 Click on these buttons to add the respective elements to your page

5 Click on this button to publish the site

GarageBand

For those who are as interested in creating music as listening to it, GarageBand can be used for this very purpose. It can take a bit of time and practice to become fully proficient with GarageBand but it is worth persevering with if you are musically inclined and want to compose your own. To use GarageBand:

1   Click on this icon on the Dock

2   Click on the New Project button

3   Give your new project a name and select a instrument with which to create it

4   Click on this button to start recording

5   Click on the instrument to record the music

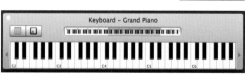

6   Click on this button to view a library of music loops which can be included in your song

7   The song is displayed in the GarageBand timeline

iCloud

Cloud computing is an attractive proposition and one that has gained greatly in popularity in recent years. As a concept, it consists of storing your content on an external computer server. This not only gives you added security in terms of backing up your information, it also means that the content can then be shared over a variety of mobile devices.

iCloud is Apple's consumer cloud computing product and one that will eventually replace the MobileMe service. This consists of online services such as email, a calendar, contacts and a photo gallery. iCloud is due to be introduced in the fall/autumn 2011 and after this MobileMe will be phased out by 2012. MobileMe users will be able to migrate to the new iCloud service, which will be free for the standard package.

iCloud will provide users with a way to save their files and apps to the online service and then use them across their mobile devices such as iPhones, iPads and iPod Touches.

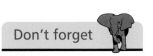

Don't forget

MobileMe users will be able to keep their current email address when they move to iCloud.

Using iCloud

iCloud will be accessible from this icon:

You can use iCloud to save and share the following:

- Music
- Photos
- Documents
- Apps
- Books
- Backups
- Contact, calendar and mail

When you save an item to the iCloud it automatically pushes it to all of your other compatible devices; you do not have to manually sync anything, iCloud does it all for you.

9 Sharing OS X

This chapter looks at how to set up different user accounts and how to keep everyone safe on your Mac using parental controls.

Adding Users

OS X enables multiple users to access individual accounts on the same computer. If there are multiple users, i.e. two or more, for a single machine, each person can sign on individually and access their own files and folders. This means that each person can log in to their own settings and preferences. All user accounts can be password protected, to ensure that each user's environment is secure. To set up multiple user accounts:

Don't forget

Every computer with multiple users has at least one main user, also known as an administrator. This means that they have greater control over the number of items that they can edit and alter. If there is only one user on a computer, they automatically take on the role of the administrator. Administrators have a particularly important role to play when computers are networked together. Each computer can potentially have several administrators.

Don't forget

Each user can select their own icon or photo of themselves.

1 Click on the System Preferences icon on the Dock

2 Click on the Users & Groups icon

3 The information about the current account is displayed. This is your own account and the information is based on details you provide when you first set up your Mac

4 Click on this icon to enable new accounts to be added (the padlock needs to be open)

5　Click on the plus sign icon to add a new account

6　Enter the details for the new account holder

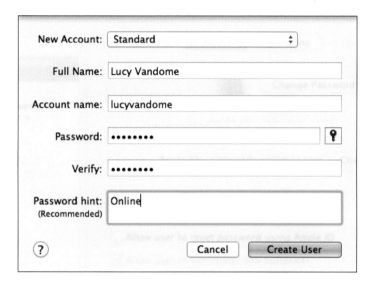

Don't forget

By default, you are the administrator of your own Mac. This means that you can administer other user accounts.

151

7　Click on the Create User button

Create User

8　The new account is added to the list in the Accounts window, under Other Accounts

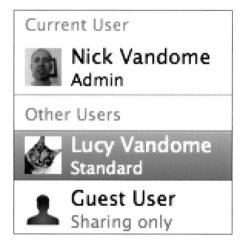

Hot tip

If an administrator forgets their password, insert the OS X CD while holding down the C key. Once this opens, select Installer>Reset Password from the Menu bar. Then select the correct user and enter a new password. Click on Save to apply the changes.

Deleting Users

Once a user has been added, their name appears on the list in the Accounts preference dialog box. It is then possible to edit the details of a particular user or delete them altogether. To do this:

Beware

Always tell other users if you are planning to delete them from the system. Don't just remove them and then let them find out the next time they try to log in. If you delete a user, their personal files are left untouched and can still be accessed.

1 Within Users & Groups, select a user from the list

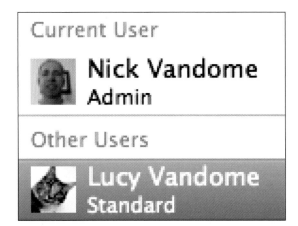

2 Click here to remove the selected person's user account

3 A warning box appears to check if you really do want to delete the selected user. If you do, select the required option and click on OK

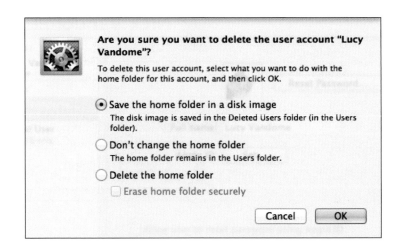

Fast User Switching

If there are multiple users using OS X it is useful to be able to switch between them as quickly as possible. When this is done, the first user's session is retained so that they can return to it if required. To switch between users:

1 In the Users & Groups window, click on the Login Options button

2 Check on the Show fast user switching menu box

3 At the top-right of the screen, click on the current user's name

Don't forget

When you switch between users, the first user remains logged in and their current session is retained intact.

4 Click on the name of another user

5 Enter the relevant password (if required)

6 Click on this button to login

153

OS X for the Family

Many families share their computers between multiple users and with the ability to create different accounts in OS X each user can have their own customized workspace. If desired, you can also set up an Apple ID so that other users can access a wider range of products, such as the Apple App Store. To do this:

1 Access Users & Groups

2 Click on the Apple ID Set... button

154

3 If the user already has an Apple ID, enter it in the appropriate box. If not click on the Create Apple ID button to create an account

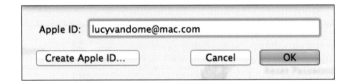

4 A page on the Apple website is accessed. This contains general information about an Apple ID and also a facility for obtaining one

Parental Controls

If children are using the computer parents may want to restrict access to certain types of information that can be viewed, using Parental Controls. To do this:

1 Access Users & Groups and click on a username and check on the Enable Parental Controls box and click on the Open Parental Controls... button

2 Click on the Apps tab

3 Check on the Use Simple Finder box to show a simplified version of the Finder

 ☑ Use Simple Finder
Provides a simplified view of the computer desktop for young or inexperienced users.

Hot tip

To check which sites have been viewed on a Web browser, check the History menu, which is located on the main Menu bar.

155

4 Check on this box if you want to limit the types of program that a user can access

5 Check off the boxes next to the programs that you do not want used

6 Click here to select options for age limits in terms of access items in the App Store

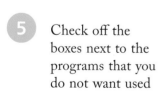

...cont'd

Web controls

1 Click on the Web tab

2 Check on this button to try to prevent access to websites with adult content

3 Check on this button to specify specific websites that are suitable to be viewed

People controls

1 Click on the People tab

2 Check on the Limit boxes to limit the type of content in email messages and iChat text messages

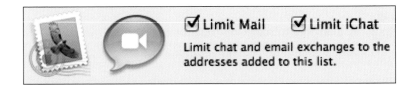

Time Limits controls

1 Click on the Time Limits tab   **Time Limits**

2 Check on this box to limit the amount of time the user can use the Mac during weekdays

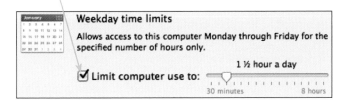

Weekday time limits

Allows access to this computer Monday through Friday for the specified number of hours only.

1 ½ hour a day

☑ Limit computer use to:

30 minutes   8 hours

3 Check on this box to limit the amount of time the user can use the Mac during weekdays

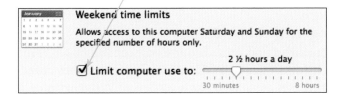

Weekend time limits

Allows access to this computer Saturday and Sunday for the specified number of hours only.

2 ½ hours a day

☑ Limit computer use to:

30 minutes   8 hours

4 Check on these boxes to determine the times at which the user cannot access their account

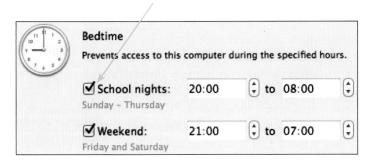

Bedtime

Prevents access to this computer during the specified hours.

☑ **School nights:**   20:00   ⬍ to 08:00   ⬍

Sunday – Thursday

☑ **Weekend:**   21:00   ⬍ to 07:00   ⬍

Friday and Saturday

OS X for Windows Users

General sharing

One of the historical complaints about Macs is that it is difficult to share files between them and Microsoft Windows computers. While this may have been true with some file types in years gone by, this is an issue that is becoming less and less important, particularly with OS X. Some of the reasons for this are:

- A number of popular file formats, such as PDFs (Portable Document Format) for documents and JPEGs (Joint Photographic Experts Group) for photos and images, are designed so that they can be used on both Mac and Windows platforms

- A lot of software programs on the Mac have options for saving files into different formats, including ones that are specifically for Windows machines

- Other popular programs, such as Microsoft Office, now have Mac versions and the resulting files can be shared on both formats

Sharing with Boot Camp

For people who find it hard to live without Microsoft Windows, help is at hand even on a Mac. Macs have a program called Boot Camp that can be used to run a version of Windows on a Mac. This is only available with Lion. Once it has been accessed, a copy of Windows can then be installed and run. This means that if you have a non-Mac program that you want to use on your Mac, you can do so with Boot Camp.

Boot Camp is set up with the Boot Camp Assistant which is located within the Utilities folder within the Applications folder. Once this is run you can then install either Windows XP, Vista or Windows 7 which will run at its native speed. If you need drivers for specific programs these can be obtained from your Lion installation disc.

Hot tip

A lot of file formats can be opened on both Macs and Windows PCs. Even Word, Excel and Powerpoint files can be exchanged, as long as each user has the relevant version of Office.

10 Advanced Features

This chapter looks at some of the more advanced capabilities of OS X such as the programming language AppleScript, the Automator and also how to share files over a network.

AppleScript

AppleScript is a programming language which can be used to write your own programs to run with OS X. These can be complex applications or they could be simple utility programs. In addition to writing your own AppleScript, OS X also comes bundled with various scripts that have already been created. These can then be used on your Mac computer. To access the AppleScript options:

Don't forget

Even for non-programmers, AppleScript is a viable option for creating simple programs within OS X.

1 In the Utilities folder, double-click on the AppleScript Editor folder

2 The AppleScript window is where the script is created

Writing Scripts

If you have some programming knowledge you may want to create your own AppleScripts. To do this:

1 Write the required AppleScript. At this point it will look like unformatted text

Don't forget

For more information about AppleScript, have a look on the website at www.macosxautomation/

2 Click on the Compile button. This will check the syntax of the script and format it according to the items that have been entered, as above

```
tell application "Finder"
    activate
    say "Hello Nick, how are you today?"
    open application "iPhoto"
    open application "Mail"
end tell
```

3   If there is a problem with the script, the Compiler will display an error message. Click OK to return to the script and correct the syntax error

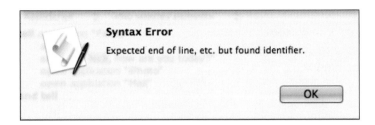

Syntax Error

Expected end of line, etc. but found identifier.

OK

4   Select File>Save from the Menu bar. Select either Script or Application as the file format

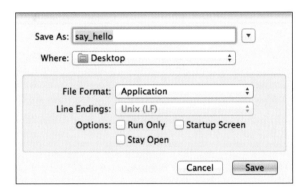

Save As: say_hello

Where: 📁 Desktop

File Format: Application

Line Endings: Unix (LF)

Options: ☐ Run Only   ☐ Startup Screen
          ☐ Stay Open

Cancel   Save

5   Click on the Save button

6   Scripts are denoted by this icon

7   Applications are denoted by this icon

say_hello

.say_hello

Using Scripts

Once scripts have been created and saved they can either be run manually or automatically.

Using scripts manually

Save the script as an application and double-click on it in its folder or add it to the Finder Sidebar and single click on it here

Don't forget

Depending on how a script has been saved as an application a dialog box may appear asking you to Run the application in order to execute it.

Using scripts automatically

1 Open System Preferences and select the Users & Groups preference. Click on the Login Items tab and click on the Plus button

Don't forget

Items can only be added to the Login by an Administrator of the Mac, usually the main user of the system.

2 Browse to the required script and select it

3 Click on the Add button to include it in the startup process. The script will then run when the computer is booted up

Automator

Automator is an OS X app that can be used to automate a series of repetitive tasks, such as renaming a folder full of images. It works by creating a workflow of tasks, which can then be applied to a specified list of folders or files. There are numerous Automator functions that are included with the application and developers are adding more constantly. To create a new workflow in Automator:

1 Double-click on this icon in the Applications folder or click on it once if it has been added to the Dock

2 Select a type of document to create and click on the Choose button

The available documents in Automator are:

- Workflow. These are a series of commands that can be run directly from the Automator

- Application. Workflows that can be run as an independent program i.e. it runs without opening Automator

- Service. Contextual workflows available throughout OS X

- Print Plugin. Workflows that run within a print dialog box

- Folder Action. Workflows that are attached to a folder in the Finder

- iCal Alarm. Workflows that are triggered by an event in iCal

- Image Capture Plugin. Workflows available in Image Capture

3 This left-hand panel contains details of applications to which certain Automator actions can be applied. Click on one to show its actions

Don't forget

Numerous actions can be added to a single workflow. However, make sure that you want all of the actions to be applied to all of the selected files or folders.

4 Select an action to add to the workflow

5 Drag the selected files into the right-hand Automator panel

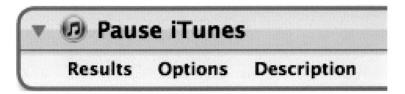

6 Click on the Run button to run the workflow

7 The Log displays whether the elements of the workflow have been successful or not

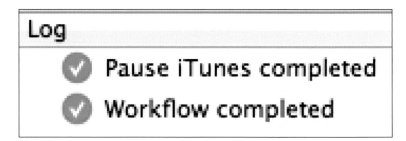

Beware

Depending on the processes involved and the number of steps, it can take a few minutes to execute an Automator workflow.

166

8 Additional actions can be added to the workflow

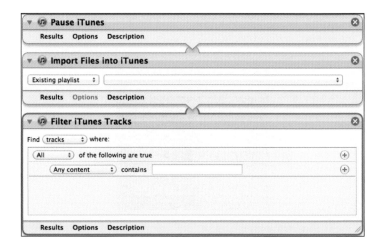

9 Any errors are displayed in the Log window

10 Once the workflow has been completed, select File>Save from the Automator Menu bar to save it. This will keep it for future use

Save As:	Pause iTunes	
Where:	📷 Desktop	
	File Format:	Workflow
		Cancel Save

11 If the document is saved as a workflow it opens up in the Automator before it can be run

12 If the document is saved as an application it runs automatically when it is activated

Networking Overview

Before you start sharing files directly between computers, you have to connect them together. This is known as networking and can be done with two computers in the same room, or with thousands of computers in a major corporation. If you are setting up your own small network it will be known in the computing world as a Local Area Network (LAN). When setting up a network there are various pieces of hardware that are initially required to join all of the required items together. Once this has been done, software settings can be applied for the networked items. Some of the items of hardware that may be required include:

- A network card. This is known as a Network Interface Card (NIC) and all recent Macs have them built-in

- An Ethernet port and Ethernet cable. This enables you to make the physical connection between devices. Ethernet cables come in a variety of forms but the one you should be looking for is the Cat5E type as this allows for the fastest transfer of data. If you are creating a wireless network then you will not require these

- A hub. This is a piece of hardware with multiple Ethernet ports that enables you to connect all of your devices together and let them communicate with each other. However, conflicts can occur with hubs if two devices try and send data through it at the same time

- A switch. This is similar in operation to a hub but it is more sophisticated in its method of data transfer, thus allowing all of the machines on the network to communicate simultaneously, unlike a hub

- A wireless router. This is for a wireless network which is increasingly the most common way to create a network. The router is connected to a telephone line and the computer then communicates with it wirelessly

Once you have worked out all of the devices that you want to include on your network you can arrange them accordingly. Try and keep the switches and hub within relative proximity of a power supply and, if you are using cables, make sure they are laid out safely.

Hot tip

If you have two Macs to be networked and they are in close proximity then this can be achieved with an Ethernet crossover cable. If you have more than two computers, then this is where an Ethernet hub is required. In either case, there is no need to connect to the Internet to achieve the network.

Ethernet network

The cheapest and easiest way to network computers is to create an Ethernet network. This involves buying an Ethernet hub or switch, which enables you to connect several devices to a central point, i.e. the hub or switch. All Apple computers and most modern printers have an Ethernet connection, so it is possible to connect various devices, not just computers. Once all of the devices have been connected by Ethernet cables, you can then start applying network settings.

AirPort network

The other option for creating a network is an AirPort network. This is a wireless network and there are two main standards used by Apple computers: AirPort, using the IEEE 802.11b standard, which is more commonly known as Wi-Fi, which stands for Wireless Fidelity and the newer AirPort Extreme, using the newer IEEE 802.11g standard which is up to 5 times faster than the older 802.11b standard. Thankfully AirPort Extreme is also compatible with devices based on the older standard, so one machine loaded with AirPort Extreme can still communicate wirelessly with an older AirPort one.

One of the issues with a wireless network is security since it is possible for someone with a wireless-enabled machine to access your wireless network, if they are within range. However, in the majority of cases the chances of this happening are fairly slim, although it is an issue about which you should be aware.

The basics of a wireless network with Macs is an AirPort card (either AirPort or AirPort Extreme) installed in all of the required machines and an AirPort base station that can be located anywhere within 150 metres of the AirPort enabled computers. Once the hardware is in place, wireless-enabled devices can be configured by using the AirPort Setup Assistant utility found in the Utilities folder. After AirPort has been set up the wireless network can be connected. All of the wireless-enabled devices should then be able to communicate with each other, without the use of a multitude of cables.

Don't forget

Another method for connecting items wirelessly is called Bluetooth. This covers much shorter distances than AirPort and is usually used for items such as printers and cellphones. Bluetooth devices can be connected by using the Bluetooth Setup Assistant in the Utilities folder.

Network Settings

Once you have connected the hardware required for a network, you can start applying the network settings that are required for different computers to communicate with one another. To do this (the following example is for networking two Mac computers):

1 In System Preferences, click on the Network button

2 For a wireless connection, click on the Turn Wi-Fi On button

Turn Wi-Fi On

3 Details of wireless settings are displayed

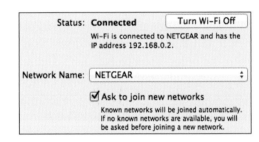

4 For a cable connection, connect an Ethernet cable

5 Details of the cable settings are displayed

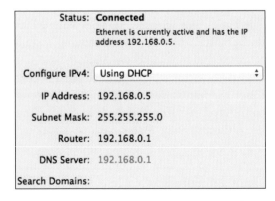

6 Click on the Advanced... button to see the full settings for each option

Advanced...

File Sharing

One of the main reasons for creating a network of two or more computers is to share files between them. On networked Macs, this involves setting them up so that they can share files and then accessing these files.

Setting up file sharing

To set up file sharing on a networked Mac:

1 Click on the System Preference button on the Dock

2 Click on the Sharing icon

3 Check on the boxes next to the items you want to share (the most common items to share are files and printers)

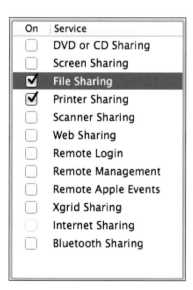

4 Click on the padlock to close it and prevent more changes

Hot tip

For OS X Lion users, files can also be shared with the AirDrop option. This can be used with two Macs that have this facility. When it is accessed, files can be shared simply by dragging them onto the icon of the other users that appears in the AirDrop window. To access AirDrop click on this button in the Finder window.

Beware

If no file sharing options are enabled in the Sharing preference window, no other users will be able to access your computer or your files, even on a network.

Hot tip

Networks can also be created between Macs and Windows-based PCs.

Connecting to a Network

Connecting as a registered user

To connect as a registered user (usually as yourself when you want to access items on another one of your own computers):

1 Other connected computers on the network will show up in the Shared section in the Finder. Click on a networked computer

2 Click on the Connect As... button

3 Check on the Registered User button and enter your username and password

4 Click on the Connect button

5 The public folders and home folder of the networked computer are available to the registered user. Double-click on an item to view its contents

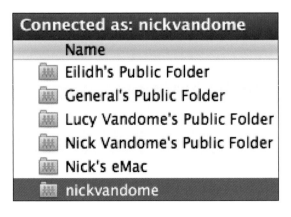

Guest users

Guest users on a network are users other than yourself, or other registered users, to whom you want to limit access to your files and folders. Guests only have access to a folder called the Drop Box in your own Public folder. To share files with Guest users you have to first copy them into the Drop Box. To do this:

1 Create a file and select File>Save from the Menu bar

2 Navigate to your own home folder (this is created automatically by OS X and displayed in the Finder Sidebar)

Beware

If another user is having problems accessing the files in your Drop Box, check the permissions settings that have been assigned to the files. See Chapter Eleven, page 186 for further details.

3 Double-click on the Public folder

Public

4 Double-click on the Drop Box folder

Drop Box

Hot tip

The contents of the Drop Box can be accessed by other users on the same computer as well as users on a network.

5 Save the file into the Drop Box

173

...cont'd

Accessing a Drop Box

To access files in a Drop Box:

 Double-click on a networked computer in the Finder

 Click on the Connect As... button in the Finder window

③ Check on the Guest button

④ Click on the Connect button

⑤ Double-click on a user's public folder

⑥ Double-click on the Drop Box folder to access the files within it

174

11 Maintaining OS X

Despite its stability OS X still benefits from a robust maintenance regime. This chapter looks at ways to keep OS X in top shape and some general troubleshooting.

Time Machine

Time Machine is a feature of OS X that gives you great peace of mind. In conjunction with an external hard drive, it creates a backup of your whole system, including folders, files, programs and even the OS X operating system itself.

Once it has been set up, Time Machine takes a backup every hour and you can then go into Time Machine to restore any files that have been deleted or become corrupt.

Setting up Time Machine

To use Time Machine it has to first be set up. This involves attaching a hard drive to your Mac. To set up Time Machine:

Beware

Make sure that you have an external hard drive that is larger than the contents of your Mac. Otherwise Time Machine will not be able to back it all up.

176

1 Click on the Time Machine icon on the Dock or access it in the System Preferences

2 You will be prompted to set up Time Machine

A storage location for Time Machine backups isn't set up.

To choose a location for backups, set up Time Machine.

(Cancel) (Set Up Time Machine)

3 Click on the Set Up Time Machine button

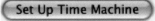

Set Up Time Machine

4 In the Time Machine System Preferences window, click on the Choose Backup Disk... button

Choose Backup Disk...

5 Connect an external hard drive and select it

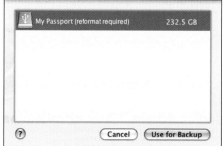

6 Click on the Use for Backup button

7 In the Time Machine System Preferences window, drag the button to the On position

8 The backup will begin. The initial backup copies your whole system and can take several hours. Subsequent hourly backups only look at items that have been changed since the previous backup

9 The progress of the backup is displayed in the System Preferences window and also here

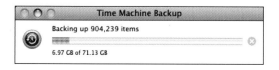

Beware

When you first set up Time Machine it copies everything on your Mac. Depending on the type of connection you have for your external drive, this could take several hours, or even days. Because of this it is a good idea to have a hard drive with a Firewire connection to make it as fast as possible.

177

Don't forget

If you stop the initial backup before it has been completed Time Machine will remember where it has stopped and resume the backup from this point.

...cont'd

Using Time Machine

Once the Time Machine has been set up it can then be used to go back in time to view items in an earlier state. To do this:

1 Access an item on your Mac and delete it. In this example IMG_2137 is deleted

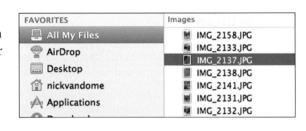

2 Click on the Time Machine icon on the Dock

3 The Time Machine displays the current item in its current state (The image is deleted). Earlier versions are stacked behind it

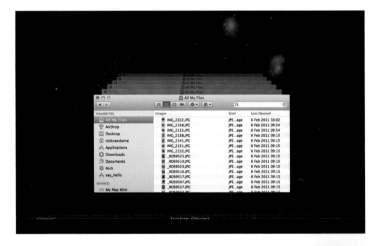

4 Click on the arrows to move through the open items or select a time or date from the scale to the right of the arrows

5 Another way to move through the Time Machine is to click on the pages behind the front one. This brings the selected item to the front. In this example Time Machine has gone back to a date when the image was still in place, i.e. before it was deleted

6 Click on the Restore button to restore the item that has been deleted

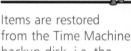

7 Click on the Cancel button to return to your normal environment

8 The deleted image is now restored in its original location

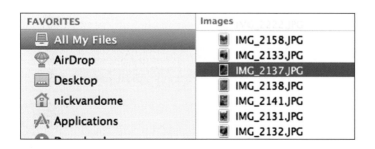

Disk Utility

Disk Utility is a utility program that allows you to perform certain testing and repair functions for OS X. It incorporates a variety of functions and it is a good option for general maintenance and if your computer is not running as it should.

Each of the functions within Disk Utility can be applied to specific drives and volumes. However, it is not possible to use the OS X start-up disk within Disk Utility as this will be in operation to run the program and Disk Utility cannot operate on a disk that has programs already running. To use Disk Utility:

Checking disks

Don't forget

If there is a problem with a disk and OS X can fix it, the Repair button will be available. Click on this to enable Disk Utility to repair the problem.

1 Click the First Aid tab to check a disk

2 Select a disk and select one of the first aid options

Erasing a disk

To erase all of the data on a disk or a volume:

Beware

If you erase data from a removable disk, such as a pen drive, you will not be able to retrieve it.

1 Click on the Erase tab and select a disk or a volume

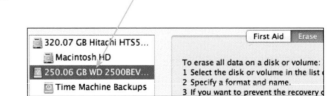

2 Click Erase to erase the data on the selected disk or volume

System Information

This can be used to view how the different hardware and software elements on your Mac are performing. To do this:

1   Open the Utilities folder and double-click on the System Information icon

2   Click on the Hardware link and click on an item of hardware

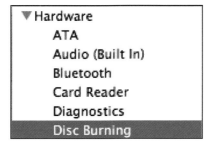

▼ **Hardware**
  ATA
  Audio (Built In)
  Bluetooth
  Card Reader
  Diagnostics
  Disc Burning

Don't forget

System Information is located within the Applications>Utilities folder.

3   Details about the item of hardware, and its performance, are displayed

MATSHITA DVD-R UJ-898:	
Firmware Revision:	HE13
Interconnect:	ATAPI
Burn Support:	Yes (Apple Shipping Drive)
Cache:	1024 KB
Reads DVD:	Yes
CD-Write:	-R, -RW
DVD-Write:	-R, -R DL, -RW, +R, +R DL, +RW
Write Strategies:	CD-TAO, CD-SAO, DVD-DAO
Media:	To show the available burn speeds, insert a disc and choose View > Refresh

4   Click on software items to view their details

Address Book	6.0
AddressBookLDAPSyncAgent	2.1

Address Book:

Version:	6.0
Last Modified:	17/06/2011 01:34
Kind:	Intel
64-Bit (Intel):	Yes
App Store:	No
Location:	/Applications/Address Book.app

Activity Monitor

Activity Monitor is a utility program that can be used to view information about how much processing power and memory are being used to run programs. This can be useful to know if certain programs are running slowly or crashing frequently. To use Activity Monitor:

 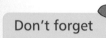
1   Click on the CPU tab to see how much processor memory is being used up

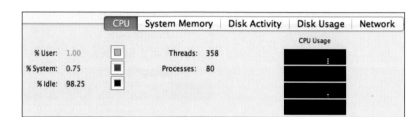

2   Click on the System Memory tab to see how much system memory (RAM) is being used up

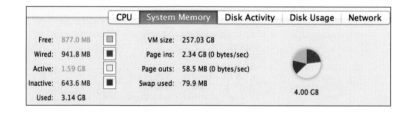

3   Click on the Disk Usage tab to see how much space has been taken up on the hard drive

Updating Software

Apple periodically releases updates for its software: both its programs and the OS X operating system. The latter are probably more important as they contain security fixes for the system that have come to light. To update software:

1 Click on the System Preferences icon on the Dock

2 Click on the Software Update icon

Software Update

3 Click on the Check Now button to view available updates

Check Now

4 Check on the boxes next to the updates you want to install

5 Click on the Install button

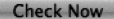

Not Now   Install 8 Items

6 Check on the Check for Updates box to have updates checked for automatically

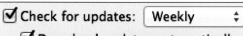

☑ Check for updates: Weekly ↕
   ☑ Download updates automatically
   You will be notified when the updates are ready to be installed.

Don't forget

In a lot of cases, software updates will be downloaded and installed automatically.

Don't forget

For some software updates, such as those to OS X itself, you may have to restart your computer for them to take effect.

Don't forget

If automatic updates is selected, you will be alerted at the appropriate time when updates are available.

Problems with Programs

The simple answer

OS X is something of a rarity in the world of computing software: it claims to be remarkably stable, and it is. However, this is not to say that things do not sometimes go wrong, although this is considerably less frequent than with older Mac operating systems. Sometimes this will be due to problems within particular programs and on occasions the problems may lie with OS X itself. If this does happen the first course of action is to close down OS X using the Apple menu>Shut Down command. Then restart the computer. If this does not work, or you cannot access the Shut Down command, try turning off the power to the computer and then starting up again.

Force quitting

If a particular program is not responding it can be closed down separately without the need to reboot the computer. To do this:

1 Select Apple menu>Force Quit from the Menu bar

2 Select the program you want to close

3 Click Force Quit

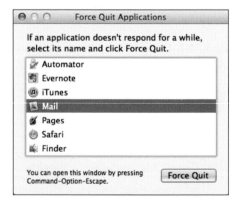

General Troubleshooting

It is true that things do go wrong with OS X, although probably with less regularity than with some other operating systems. If something does go wrong, there are a number of items that you can check and also some steps you can take to ensure that you do not lose any important data if the worst case scenario occurs and your hard drive packs up completely.

- **Backup**. If everything does go wrong it is essential to take preventative action in the form of making sure that all of your data is backed up and saved. This can either be done with the Backup program available from the .Mac service or by backing up manually by copying data to a CD or DVD

- **Reboot**. One traditional reply by IT helpdesks is to reboot, i.e. turn off the computer and turn it back on again and hope that the problem has resolved itself. In a lot of cases this simple operation does the trick but it is not always a viable solution for major problems

- **Check cables**. If the problem appears to be with a network connection or an externally connected device, check that all cables are connected properly and have not worked loose. If possible, make sure that all cables are tucked away so that they cannot inadvertently be pulled out

- **Check network settings**. If your network or Internet connections are not working, check the network setting in System Preferences. Sometimes when you make a change to one item this can have an adverse effect on one of these settings. (If possible, lock the settings once you have applied them, by clicking on the padlock icon in the Network preferences window)

- **Check for viruses**. If your computer is infected with a virus this could affect the efficient running of the machine. Luckily this is less of a problem for Macs as virus writers tend to concentrate their efforts towards Windows-based machines. However, there are plenty of Mac viruses out there, so make sure your computer is protected by a program such as Norton AntiVirus which is available from www.symantec.com

...cont'd

● **Check Start-up items**. If you have set certain items to start automatically when your computer is turned on, this could cause certain conflicts within your machine. If this is the case, disable the items from launching during the booting up of the computer. This can be done within the Accounts preference of System Preferences by clicking on the Startup Items tab, selecting the relevant item and pressing the minus button

● **Check permissions**. If you, or other users, are having problems opening items this could be because of the permissions that are set. To check these, select the item in the Finder, click on the File button on the Finder toolbar and select Get Info. In the Ownership & Permissions section of the Info window you will be able to set the relevant permissions to allow other users, or yourself, to read, write or have no access

Click here to view permissions settings

● **Eject external devices**. Sometimes external devices, such as pen drives, can become temperamental and refuse to eject the disks within them, or even show up on the desktop or in the Finder. If this happens you can eject the disk by pressing the mouse button when the Mac chimes are heard during the booting up process

● **Turn off your screen saver**. Screen savers can sometimes cause conflicts within your computer, particularly if they have been downloaded from an unreliable source. If this happens, change the screen saver within the Desktop & Screen Saver preference of the System Preferences or disable it altogether

Index